Praise fo

D0198460

"For a large part of my life, fear ratt   w the pain. *Unafraid,* by Carey Scott, is not only a heart-engaging read, it is hope, healing, and a healthy dose of courage for those ready to be good-and-done with fear."

—Kelly Balarie, author of *Fear Fighting* and *Battle Ready: Train Your Mind to Conquer Challenges, Defeat Doubt, and Live Victoriously,* national speaker and blogger at purposefulfaith.com

"*Unafraid* is for every person who craves an authentic life but is unsure of how to practically step into that space. I appreciate Carey's honest awareness, insight, and biblical wisdom. I closed the final page feeling free to live unafraid of who God made me to be. You will too. Plus Carey is hilarious, and authenticity and humor are pretty much the makings of a perfect read. #blessitall"

—Bekah Pogue, author of *Choosing REAL* book and devotional, speaker, spiritual director in training, writer at bekahpogue.com

"The thing about Carey Scott is that she is entirely real. Fear is the enemy's cheapest trick. As someone who has fallen prey to the terror, from a fear of death, heights, spiders, vomit, and egg salad—as well as fear of being who God created me to be—Carey's words are pure freedom. Out of the deepest dungeons, read this. . .and step into the light."

—Jami Amerine, author of *Stolen Jesus* and *Sacred Ground, Sticky Floors,* speaker and writer at SacredGroundStickyFloors.com

"*Unafraid* is a bold conversation about identity that we, as women, need to participate in. Carey walks with us through the feelings of too much and not enough, all the while challenging us to recognize that the unique person God created us to be is someone of incredible value and worth. Thank you, Carey, for empowering us to shine!"

—Bobbie Schaeperkoetter, Founder of Build A Sister Up, Co-Founder of That Upcycled Life, and host of TUL Uncut, writer at Bobbieschae.com

Dedication

To the woman too afraid to be herself...

To the woman worried that who
she truly is isn't good enough...

To the woman hiding her authentic
self from everyone around her...

this book is dedicated to you.

I was you. I am you sometimes even now.

And I pray this book offers a compelling reason
to be confident in who God created you to be.

I pray you choose to be authentic no matter what.

I pray you accept your awesomeness every day.

I pray you live unafraid to be *you.*

un-afraid

BE YOU. BE AUTHENTIC.

FIND THE GRIT AND GRACE TO SHINE.

CAREY SCOTT

SHILOH RUN  PRESS

An Imprint of Barbour Publishing, Inc.

Scripture quotations marked VOICE are taken from The Voice™. Copyright © 2008 by Ecclesia Bible Society. Used by permission. All rights reserved.

Scripture quotations marked MSG are from *THE MESSAGE.* Copyright © by Eugene H. Peterson 1993, 1994, 1995, 1996, 2000, 2001, 2002. Used by permission of NavPress Publishing Group.

Scripture quotations marked TLB are taken from The Living Bible © 1971. Used by permission of Tyndale House Publishers, Inc. Wheaton, Illinois 60189. All rights reserved.

Scripture quotations marked GNT are taken from the Good News Translation® (Today's English Standard Version, Second Edition), Copyright © 1992 American Bible Society. All rights reserved.

Scripture quotations marked AMP are taken from the Amplified® Bible, © 2015 by The Lockman Foundation. Used by permission.

Scripture quotations marked AMPC are taken from the Amplified® Bible, Classic Edition © 1954, 1958, 1962, 1964, 1965, 1987 by The Lockman Foundation. Used by permission.

Scripture quotations marked NIV are taken from the HOLY BIBLE, NEW INTERNATIONAL VERSION®. NIV®. Copyright © 1973, 1978, 1984, 2011 by Biblica, Inc.™ Used by permission. All rights reserved worldwide.

Scripture quotations marked GW are taken from GOD'S WORD®, © 1995 God's Word to the Nations. Used by permission of Baker Publishing Group.

Scripture quotations marked NKJV are taken from the New King James Version®. Copyright © 1982 by Thomas Nelson, Inc. Used by permission. All rights reserved.

Scripture quotations marked NOG are taken from the Names of God Bible (NOG) The Names of God Bible (without notes) © 2011 by Baker Publishing Group.

Scripture quotations marked TPT are from The Passion Translation®. Copyright © 2017 by BroadStreet Publishing® Group, LLC. Used by permission. All rights reserved. ThePassionTranslation.com.

Cover: Greg Jackson, Thinkpen Design

Published in association with Jessica Kirkland and the literary agency of Kirkland Media Management, LLC, P.O. Box 1539, Liberty, Texas 77575.

Published by Shiloh Run Press, an imprint of Barbour Publishing, Inc., 1810 Barbour Drive, Uhrichsville, Ohio 44683, www.shilohrunpress.com

Our mission is to inspire the world with the life-changing message of the Bible.

Member of the
Evangelical Christian
Publishers Association

Printed in the United States of America.

Acknowledgments

A huge thank-you to my husband and kids. I could never do what I do without you. Not only do you give me excellent material to write and speak about, but you challenge me to walk out the words I write every day. My hope is that my life encourages you to love the Lord your God with all your heart, with all your soul, with all your strength, and with all your mind.

Sam and Sara, I absolutely love being your mom—a privilege I'll never take for granted. I adore everything about you, and my heart could not be more full of love for you both. And, Wayne, I'm so grateful to walk this adventure alongside you. What a beautiful family we've created. You're deeply loved. You three are my greatest joys.

Jessie Kirkland, my amazing literary agent and friend, more than anyone else you've helped me traverse these past few years. Your constant belief in me has helped me be unafraid to stand up for my person, my calling, and my work. We've logged countless hours on the phone, standing together through some daunting seasons of life. I deeply appreciate you on so many levels. And the authenticity we've developed in our friendship is nothing short of beautiful.

To my friends—Lisa, Janet, Sherry, Cat, Tracy, Megan, Bobbie, Amanda, Bebe, Lindsey—thank you for the coffee/lunch/dinner dates, phone calls, text messages, emails, and hilarious Snapchats. You've lifted my spirits more than a few times and boldly reminded me that who I am is good. You've challenged me to dig for the grit to hold on and the grace to be nice when I wanted to be snarky. Thank you for giving me courage to be me. You girls are gifts.

Kelly McIntosh, Shalyn Sattler, and the entire team at Barbour Publishing, you're truly a pleasure to work with! Thank you for another opportunity to share my words with others and for believing in me once again. Your support and expertise are greatly appreciated.

And to you, the courageous one holding this book right now, I'm so glad you're here. Thank you for listening to the Holy Spirit's prompting to pick up *Unafraid*. The world needs everything you were created to bring into it, and I'm praying that God gives you the courage you need through the words on these pages. That you would share your precious time with me means everything. Together, let's learn how to #beUnafraid so we can #beAuthentic.

Contents

CHAPTER 1

The Case for Fake

One of the greatest regrets in life is being what others
would want you to be, rather than being yourself.
Shannon L. Alder[1]

All the money is gone. This was the final answer at the end of a long line of questions.

This trio of sisters had been sharing responsibility for their dad ever since their mom died, leaving the details of his finances and medical care in their hands. The sisters weren't exactly tight, but they each played a part in their father's care. It wasn't easy as two of them were out-of-state, and many times I had sat with my friend as she cried over the frustrations that came with this arrangement. But it was working. And this father was one of the sweetest people I'd ever known. I loved him like he was part of my own family. He was kind and loving.

And trusting.

Eventually my friend saw some red flags—a few areas

that seemed concerning—from the sister handling all the finances. She'd also received tips from concerned family members that things weren't adding up. She struggled to imagine how her Spidey senses and the whistle-blowers' accusations could be true, and when she confronted the sister in question, her explanations seemed solid. Life went back to normal.

These sisters had grown up together, had spent countless holidays together, had shared big family vacations together, and had connected often through phone and email. I knew this family, and I had seen throughout the years how important family was to each of them. So when my friend felt certain these allegations couldn't possibly be true, I believed that too. But soon more red flags began to wave.

I walked through those painfully revealing days with my friend. I watched well-crafted stories unravel. I was there when this family began to uncover the horrible truth that had been going on for years. And I wept when the sister's lies were exposed. She had been living anything but an authentic life.

They discovered a tangled web of lies, counterfeit living that had marked most of her adult life. This was the sister who had graduated from seminary, led youth groups, and spoken from a stage. She was a favorite among the nieces and nephews. This one ran in well-known circles. And she had stolen every bit of money her father had—every last penny. New credit cards had been opened. Debt had piled up. Medical insurance had been canceled. Savings had been spent. Investments had been drained. It was all gone.

In this sister's mind, she justified being inauthentic with those she claimed to love. She made up reasons for lying to those who trusted her the most. And somehow she decided living fake felt safer than being honest about financial troubles. Living fake felt better than admitting failure. Living fake felt easier than finding the courage to be honest and upright and selfless. She bought into the case for fake. And it eventually cost this sister her life.

My friend graciously allowed me to share this part of her story with you, and out of respect for the continued heartache and healing of her family, I won't go into more detail. But you know what? I have my own whack-a-doo stories about family members choosing to live fake. I'm learning that these kinds of stories aren't that rare. Chances are someone in your own family tree has chosen counterfeit living instead of standing brave for truth.

But even worse, I can think of times I've lived fake—times I've been too ashamed or afraid of being myself. I have been in relationships where I didn't think my genuine feelings and thoughts mattered, so I hid them. I've wanted to speak out for an injustice but was too scared of criticism. Instead, I went along with the groupthink.

I think of seasons in my life when I was dying inside, battling demons from some childhood abuse, but I didn't ask for help. I grinned and bore it alone. Or times I felt over-whelmed and underwater but acted like everything was fine. And I can remember times I sat in silence or even joined into conversations with women being mean-spirited in their gossip. Even though I felt the Holy Spirit's prompting to speak up or walk away, I was afraid of ridicule.

I've acted more important than I really am. I've let others think I was more together than was true. I've pretended instead of being honest. I've been hypocritical rather than genuine. I've been dishonest rather than risk my reputation. And that's just scratching the surface.

If you've read my other two books—*Untangled* and *Uncommon*—you'll know I'm pretty transparent with my life and my story. I believe there's power in testimony, so I'm an advocate for authenticity. Oh yes, I love diving into the deep waters of intimacy with conversations that reveal the heart. And from the stage, I try to challenge women to be real with themselves, others, and God. I haven't always been that way.

The Lord and I have done some work over the past several years—work that has given me the courage and confidence to be okay with who I am. This is a new way of living, and it has taken grit and grace to walk it out. Most of my life, it felt safer to live fake. In my insecurities, I chose to be phony. Fear told me to be deceptive, hiding the truth of who I really was instead of shining. But with each baby step out of the shadows of counterfeit living, I've seen the beauty of imperfection.

We need to cover one big reality now, because it will help us answer the "why" when we struggle to live authentic, not fake. I don't know about you, but I'm all in until things get crunchy. I'm sold out until the straight path begins to wind and point uphill. Those are the times I want to quit and go back to the status quo—back to hiding the real me from the world. It's when I end up asking myself, *Why am I advocating for authenticity?*

So let me start by stating the obvious. Ready?

Living fake is so much easier than living authentic. (Mic drop)

Here's why. To live the authentic life means we choose to believe we are who God says we are, not who we've been told we should be by other people or cultural standards. It means our words and actions mirror our beliefs and values. We're going to unpack this in detail in the next chapter, but can we agree here and now that being real is hard to do?

And chances are you're presenting a counterfeit you right now and don't even realize it. It's not always a choice we consciously make, you know. Sometimes it's a defense mechanism to keep the hurt away. It's a habit we've picked up courtesy of the school of hard knocks. Other times it's what we were modeled growing up and it became our normal. It can also be part of our God-given temperament, especially when we're introverted or shy. And for many of us, we learned a long time ago that opening up and letting someone in sets us up for heartache, so we've chosen to present a more controlled exterior that rarely reflects our interior.

Let's think about it. How many times has someone asked how you are, and you've quickly responded, "I'm fine," or "Everything's great." Your marriage may be falling apart, but at Bible study you smile and act like life is just dandy. When you meet a friend for coffee, you talk recipes and Black Friday shopping strategies instead of sharing the deep fears you have about parenting. You might be drowning in debt, but no one has any idea you're in over your head. As far as anyone else can tell, your life couldn't get any better even if you tried.

Somewhere along the way, you decided not to share the real you with the world. You thought to yourself, *It's just easier this way. It spares my feelings. It cuts down on drama. And I don't have to justify or defend myself.* Maybe you think you're not worth knowing, and rather than let your insecurities get all tangled up, you bailed on authentic living. Maybe fear of criticism or judgment got in the way. Maybe you have a long memory of times you opened up and it didn't go so well. Oh my gosh, I get it. Fake feels safer and easier. Yes and amen. And you know what? Sometimes it just might be wisdom.

It's not realistic to think we should be ready and willing to verbally vomit our innermost pain all over someone when they ask how we're doing. We may be a hot mess, but there is a time and place to open up and share. We don't have to walk around in tears every day when we're in a tough season. Sometimes we just have to put on our lipstick and mascara and find a way to *adult*. Right? Again, there is a time and place. And we don't always have to call someone out or get all heated up the moment our feelings get hurt. For Pete's sake, we don't have to attend every fight we're invited to. We can choose to extend grace or approach the other party in honesty once we've calmed down.

The truth is many of us may need a big dose of discernment so we know when sharing our true thoughts and feelings is a good thing. We must navigate a balance. But here's where the problem lies. Many of us never seem to find the *right* time or motivation to open up and reveal the true us. (Geez, I didn't for years.) Instead, we keep our authentic selves locked away and live our socially acceptable selves instead. We settle for fake because it's easier and safer.

I remember opening up to a friend about something that had hurt my feelings deep down. It was the knock-me-to-my-knees kind of hurt, and I was still trying to catch my breath from it. I hadn't really shared what happened with anyone until I did with her because I was still processing it. And as I unpacked the details of the event, I wept. I really let my friend peek inside my heart. It felt so vulnerable and a little scary, but my protective walls had come down, and I didn't have the wherewithal to pull myself together at that point. It was an ugly-cry moment.

And then she said, "If God brought you to it, He'll bring you through it." Can I be honest? I almost punched her. Seriously, people. We have to stop using these kinds of Christian platitudes on each other. They may look great on a social media graphic, but few things will shut down authenticity faster. Same with quoting scripture. These platitudes do not often work well in those honest moments, girls. And this was one of those moments.

Now, I love God's Word and encouraging phrases as much as the next person, but here is some advice: When someone gives you the privilege of seeing the depth of their heart, consider it sacred ground. They usually aren't looking for guidance or for you to minimize their hurt with cute sayings or slogans. They need someone to listen as they purge their heart. They need a cry buddy or someone to give a hug when they need it the most.

You've just been invited into a beautiful moment of authenticity. Embrace it, because when you offer someone room to be messy and real without judgment or fix-it answers, that's one of the greatest gifts you can ever offer another human being. And it can be a touchstone memory of why they don't have to live fake.

Well I didn't punch my friend, nor did I tell her she handled it all wrong. But I'll be honest, that experience will make me think twice before opening up to her again. Her intention might have been good, but her response to my honesty was an authenticity killer. It encouraged the real me to stay tucked away without even meaning to. And worse, hers was the kind of response that helps make the case for fake.

But you know what just might be one of the most compelling reasons counterfeit living seems like a viable option? *Shame.*

Shame keeps us from being authentic because it says who we are is not okay. Deep down, we believe the *real* us is unacceptable, so we present another version—one that looks less messy and more put together. Shame weaves its way into our self-worth, reminding us of all the times we put ourselves out there and didn't measure up. Shame makes us remember moments we've shared the depths of our heart and were met with ridicule or judgment. It sucks the life out of us. Shame makes a strong case for fake living.

You know what else? Shame gives us an honesty hangover. Do you know what I mean? It's the feeling we shared too much. . .we looked too messy or too needy. . .we didn't sound gracious enough. . .we were unfair with our words . . .we sounded too full of ourselves. . .we talked too much. Shame hits us hard after we open up with our honest feelings and whispers, "You are ridiculous." Yep, shame has a way of telling us we're either not enough or too much.

When shame tangles me, I usually tuck away. I hide from community because I'm embarrassed by what I've done or who I am. Sometimes shame makes me feel like a scared little cat backed into a corner, and I come out attacking like a lion. Yeah, that's not pretty. But mostly I sit and ruminate over my failures and shortcomings. This creates self-doubt and knocks my confidence, but I try to look unshaken. And as I'm curled up in bed nursing my wounded heart, I watch one of my favorite chick flicks and cry for the hundredth time.

Now it's your turn. How does shame discourage authentic

living for you? Write it out here:

_____

_____

_____

_____

_____

_____

_____

_____

_____

_____

_____

Shame is real, it's powerful, and it has stolen so much, yet God is ready to remove it so you can live authentic. He wants to heal anything keeping you from being you. Your Father is ready to free you up to be who He created you to be, because He's not for counterfeit living. His plan was never for you to live tucked away, hiding in your *I'm not good enough* feelings. God wants you to stand in His truth, living authentic and unwilling to conform to the world's unreasonable standards.

Be comforted in knowing you're not alone when it comes to fighting fear about being yourself. We're all in this together. Even back in Bible times, living without shame was a struggle—a challenge with only one answer. "But Lord, you are my shield, my glory, and my only hope. *You alone* can lift my head, now bowed in shame" (Psalm 3:3 TLB, emphasis mine).

It's so human to be afraid of living authentic. It's scary to unbelieve the messages shame has whispered into your soul.

It takes real grit to be honest about who you are and what you think. It takes guts to stand up and speak out for what you believe. And it takes grace to navigate it all. But I want you to know it matters, and God sees every choice you make to be real in a world that glorifies the fake. He alone will be your shield, your victory, and your hope.

In John 8, we meet a woman whose story can speak directly to this truth. My heart can barely handle the amount of embarrassment she must have felt. I hurt for her. I'm humiliated on her behalf. I can only imagine how uncomfortable she must have been in that moment. And honestly, the way she was treated makes me so angry. Let me set the stage.

Waking up early, Jesus left the Mount of Olives and made His way to the temple in Jerusalem. As He arrived and attracted a crowd, He sat down and started teaching. Can we stop here for a minute? I am so in awe of Jesus' willingness to shift gears. He was heading for the temple and allowed the needs of the people to distract Him. Soak that in for a sec. Girls, I am graceless pre-coffee, so this act of kindness blows me away—especially so early in the morning.

Now visualize this impromptu church service. Can you see the crowd sitting and standing around Jesus, hanging on His every word? Can you imagine how quiet it was as they listened with intensity to what Jesus was sharing? What a beautiful moment in time, right? And then that sacred space was interrupted.

I'm sure the crowd was caught off guard at the commotion coming their way. Within moments, a woman was standing in front of Jesus. The scribes and Pharisees had dragged her from the adulterous bed, and there she stood, facing the Messiah. We don't know what she was wearing or how presentable she was, but we can assume she was not at her best.

I'm also sure she was scared, knowing she had committed a crime. She had to be sad, knowing this was how her life had turned out. She may have been angry that the man sharing her bed was assigned no blame in this situation. But I can *guarantee* you she was covered in shame, embarrassed about who she was.

I want to have coffee with this woman in heaven. I want to hug her neck and tell her how much I appreciate her story. Shame kept me living fake for so long, and her story of redemption has been an encouragement. She wasn't living as her authentic self—no one is born with the desire to have extramarital affairs—and it was an encounter with Jesus that gave her courage to be real. Those words stand true for us today.

Now let's grab our front-row seat and watch this powerful exchange unfold between Jesus, her accusers, and this embarrassed-beyond-belief woman scared straight out of her mind. You can find her story documented in John 8:4–11 (VOICE).

> **Pharisees:** *Teacher, this woman was caught in the act of adultery. Moses says in the law that we are to kill such women by stoning. What do You say about it?*
> *This was all set up as a test for Jesus; His answers would give them grounds to accuse Him of crimes against Moses' law. Jesus bent over and wrote something in the dirt with His finger. They persisted in badgering Jesus, so He stood up straight.*

Jesus: Let the first stone be thrown by the one among you who has not sinned.

Once again Jesus bent down to the ground and resumed writing with His finger. The Pharisees who heard Him stood still for a few moments and then began to leave slowly, one by one, beginning with the older men. Eventually only Jesus and the woman remained, and Jesus looked up.

Jesus: Dear woman, where is everyone? Are we alone? Did no one step forward to condemn you?

***Woman Caught in Adultery:** Lord, no one has condemned me.*

Jesus: Well, I do not condemn you either; all I ask is that you go and from now on avoid the sins that plague you.

Don't skip over these wonderful words, because they are life-giving. *Jesus doesn't condemn.* He does not berate us for our sins. And listen to this. *Merriam-Webster's Dictionary* defines the verb *condemn* as "saying in a strong and definite way that someone is bad or wrong."[2] That's the very essence of shame. Even more, God has no part in spreading condemnation.

Remember, shame is feeling unhappy with who you are as a person. It's believing that at your very core you're bad and inherently flawed. When Jesus told this woman tangled up in her shame and exposed by her sin that even the God of the universe does not condemn her, her life was forever changed. That's revolutionary love and acceptance right there. And you know what? Get this. It's available to you and me right now.

But just like the adulterous woman from John 8, you and I have existed in counterfeit ways. We've made choices that don't reflect who God created us to be. Our words and actions haven't revealed the truth of who we really are. And for far too long, we've justified living fake because it has just felt easier and safer. Shame has held us hostage, unable to see that who we are is good.

The truth is authentic living costs us something.

It costs us intentionality. It costs us vulnerability. It costs us comfortability. It forces us to muster the grit to trust again, being willing to put ourselves out there one more time. Authentic living requires grace to have realistic expectations for ourselves and others, and it necessitates a huge dose of confidence and courage so we can shine. This kind of living is the result of spending time with Jesus.

Yes, authentic living costs you something. But, friend, when we choose it over the counterfeit life, something beautiful happens. When we each decide to live and love the way we were created to live and love, we look like the church. Listen to this from Romans 12:3–8 in The Voice translation.

> *Because of the grace allotted to me, I can respectfully tell you not to think of yourselves as being more important than you are; devote your minds to sound judgment since God has assigned to each of us a measure of faith. For in the same way that one body has so many different parts, each with* different functions; *we, too—the many—are* different parts *that* form one body *in the Anointed One. Each one of us is* joined *with one another, and* we become together what we could not be alone. *Since our gifts vary depending on the grace poured out on each of us, it is important that* we exercise the gifts we have been given. *If prophecy is your gift, then speak*

a prophet according to your proportion of faith. If
[ser]vice is your gift, then serve well. If teaching is your
gift, then teach well. If you have been given a voice of
encouragement, then use it often. If giving is your gift,
then be generous. If leading, then be eager to get started.
If sharing God's mercy, then be cheerful in sharing it.
(emphasis mine)

I know, that's a lot of words in a long paragraph. Sometimes I see a big block of copy and get overwhelmed, so I skim it. But let's pick this apart together to find the gold nuggets, okay?

This passage reveals some awesome details about why choosing to live authentic is so necessary, even though it's hard. Paul is. . .

- confirming we each have a specific call (mission, purpose, gifting) to walk out in our lifetime,
- reminding us that along with that call comes the faith we need to make it happen,
- saying our different callings are designed to work together with other Jesus followers, and
- encouraging us to be our true selves and share our God-given gifts because doing it creates a stronger community that can accomplish more.

So if we decide *not to embrace* our calling, choose to disagree with who God created us to be, continue living counterfeit lives, and opt out of community, everyone around us will miss out on what we could have brought to the table.

Our fear of being real will let others down. It will neuter our effectiveness for the Kingdom. And it will tell our Creator that we don't like His handiwork (*Psst.* None of these are good.)

Let's make a change. Heck, let's *be* the change. Isn't there enough insincerity and dishonesty in the world? If you're anything like me, making a case for fake isn't hard. Gosh, we've been doing it for years. There's no arguing it's the safe and easy choice. But it's not working, and our hearts are craving authentic connections with others. We're yearning to be seen and known. And our passion to be real with God is burning.

Let's make authentic living in the name of Jesus cool again. Are you with me?

CHAPTER 2

This Is
Authentic Living

*Authenticity is a collection of choices that we have to
make every day. It's about the choice to show up and be real.
The choice to be honest. The choice to let our true selves be seen.*
—Brené Brown[3]

Authentic living. What does it even mean?

It's a confusing idea, honestly. Authenticity is one of those Christianese buzz phrases that weave their way through our conversations almost daily. People write about authentic living, preachers preach on it, and it's what we Jesus-girls strive for. I think most of us want to live that way. We want to have community that values candidness, but we may also recognize that walking out vulnerability isn't always easy.

Sometimes it's hard to negotiate the line between being real and being *too* real. We don't always know how to navigate being honest about our feelings and being oversharers.

And we may struggle to find the grit and grace to create transparent relationships when sharing our heart has back-fired in the past—more than once.

These days it feels like authenticity has been misused, misinterpreted, and watered down. And instead of trying to live out this worthy pursuit in ways that honor us, esteem others, and glorify God, we've made a hot mess of it all. Authentic living has lost its potency.

But I still crave it. Maybe, since you're holding this book in your hands, you do too.

Something about a deep-water discussion invigorates my heart. To be honest, I don't care what you had for dinner. I'm not interested in the latest sale at the mall. I don't want to share recipes, talk about the weather, gossip about some-one's life, or gab about what's happening on that television show. But if you want to know what is tugging on my heart, if you want an update on where God is working in my life, if you need to talk through the joys and struggles of parenting and share how I can pray for your marriage. . .I'm all in.

To me, this is what authentic living looks like.

In a world where fake is the name of the game, we're losing the battle for true, authentic living. And one of the main reasons is that we're simply too afraid to be real.

I know a woman who sells a specific line of clothes out of her home. Thanks to online promotion through social media, she's making enough money to pay down their hefty medical bills. She's masterful in how she presents herself on Facebook, sharing the perfect mixture of personal tidbits, parenting humor, and business talk. To all who follow her, she presents an all-together woman with an all-together life. But it's not true.

At coffee one morning, she sat in a puddle of tears across the table from me. Her world was so messy—struggling marriage, troubled daughter, and medical insurance woes. She was pouring out her heart until another friend unexpectedly walked into the coffee shop and over to our table. Within moments, she went from the deep valley of depression to the high hilltop of happy. And when this friend—a woman she hangs out with regularly—asked if she had been crying, she blamed her tears on a lack of sleep and hormones.

I sat stunned.

When her friend's coffee order arrived, they waved goodbye and promised to touch base later that week. I turned and asked, "Why didn't you tell your friend the truth? She loves you." Her response to my question was real and raw. And it was so gritty and gut-wrenchingly honest that I hugged her neck tight. She said, "I can't share those struggles with her. She has an easy marriage, perfect kids, and more money than she knows what to do with. There is no way she could relate to what I'm going through."

That experience made me realize that not only is the concept of authenticity confusing, but with it comes painful memories of times when *being real* has punched us right in the gut. Times we've felt embarrassed, and it's knocked our confidence. Times we've been tangled in insecurities about who we are, vowing not to let our crazy show again. Times we've felt stupid because no one has seemed to understand. Times we've poured out the depths of our heart to someone and they've criticized and ridiculed when what we really needed was an "Aw, honey" response. Times we spoke up about how we felt and the hammer of judgment dropped hard on us.

Times like those have left us wondering if it's even worth it. I mean, why be authentic when it feels like a setup for heartache?

I get it. I really do. Sometimes it's a huge struggle to muster the guts and grit to put yourself out there one more time. It's hard to live authentically in a world that doesn't see the value in it. And when your heart gets stomped on again and again and again, at some point you raise the white flag and decide to keep the real you covered up. It feels safer and easier.

So instead of being authentic, you fake it. You grin and bear it. You act like nothing bothers you. You roll with the punches. You act like an easygoing kind of girl. You go with the flow. You keep your opinions to yourself. But, friend, that's not who you are meant to be.

God didn't create you without a voice. He didn't design you to be a *yes girl,* keeping the Holy Spirit's promptings silenced. Your Father in heaven didn't fashion you as a unique, one-of-a-kind rock star just to have you try to blend in. No. He made you to stand out. He made you matchless. You are irreplaceable. Embracing counterfeit living was never part of God's plan.

It's time to embrace authenticity. And not only do we need to live that way, but God wants us to encourage others to do the same. It's time to find our resolve to be real. We need to muster confidence so we can overcome fear and be who God created us to be. We need to ask Him for the grit and grace to be our true selves.

Maybe it's a good idea to define and unpack a few words and phrases here: *grit, grace, authentic living,* and *counterfeit living.* We need a firm footing as we traverse the roads of authentic living. Here we go.

GRIT

When I think of this word, I see an image of people's faces covered in sweat and dirt. Their breathing is rapid, like they've been running or wrestling. There's no doubt they've been working hard at something, and it hasn't been a cakewalk. But they have the eye of the tiger. They're in it to win it. And rather than hang their heads in defeat, they're staring down their challengers. They won't give up until they win.

Doesn't that image get your gears going? I'm thinking Mel Gibson in the movie *Braveheart*, Sandra Bullock in *The Blind Side*, Daniel Day Lewis in *The Last of the Mohicans*, Scarlett Johansson as Black Widow in *The Avengers*, Liam Neeson in *Taken*, or even Sylvester Stallone in *Rocky*. Sweet mother, these characters weren't giving up.

Having grit means you have passion and perseverance to do something even though difficulties and distractions are in your way. This is a stick-to-it mentality. It's what keeps you moving forward when it would be easier to give up. Grit is what makes you get back in the saddle rather than walk away in defeat. And it's what allows you to stay engaged rather than give up or quit.

People with grit allow failure to ignite them to grow and learn for the next time around. They realize they're in a marathon, not a sprint. And having grit means they're determined, willing to work hard for the result. Even more, gritty people are content with delayed gratification. They don't need immediate resolution because the long journey ahead doesn't intimidate them.

Yes, having grit means you are one brave soul. It means you are full of courage and tenacity. And I love everything about this word.

GRACE

Grace is a beautiful mixture of kindness, compassion, favor, and love, and you and I didn't earn it or deserve it. And grace isn't limited by conditions that must be met. In other words, we don't have to have a perfect response, the right behavior, or a flawless performance. These factors have nothing to do with grace. Praise the Lord, right?

In Jesus-girl words, it means we're loved when we're unlovable. Who you are or what you do doesn't matter. It's favor extended. Grace saves us (Ephesians 2:8). Grace helps us win the battle against sin (James 4:6). Grace is a gift to us (Ephesians 4:7). And grace is at the very core of the Gospel (Acts 20:24).

But in the context of our discussion, I want to focus more on giving ourselves grace. Listen, we need to stop partnering with self-contempt. When did we decide our perfection was expected? Part of what makes this journey beautiful is discovering grace for the ups and downs of authentic living. It's freeing ourselves from guilt when we mess up. It's telling ourselves *it's okay* when we try and fail or accidentally fall back into old habits.

Giving ourselves grace is refusing to get on the performance treadmill that says we must be perfect. You and I are not flawless. Never have been, never will be. Let's settle that right here and now. Knowing that truth helps us be prepared to extend grace and forgive ourselves for shortcomings, bad choices, and wrong decisions.

We must find both grit and grace to live authentic—no doubt about it. These two go hand in hand as we pursue truth-based lives where we can be the real us.

Now let's dig into the guts of what authentic living looks like.

AUTHENTIC LIVING

According to the dictionary,[4] *authentic* means:

- not false or copied; genuine; real
- representing one's true nature or beliefs; true to oneself
- having an origin supported by unquestionable evidence; authenticated; verified

Oh my gosh, girl. This is pretty amazing. Did you notice these three definitions perfectly describe three different beneficiaries of your authenticity? Here's what I mean:

1. This is how we are to be with others. *Real and genuine.*
2. This is how we are to be with ourselves. *True and honest.*
3. This is how we are to be with God. *Believing we are who He says we are.*

I love when God blows my mind like this. I love when He gives me those powerful *aha* moments! And I love when I geek out on a string of words and my inner nerd comes out. Anyway, back to my point.

Isn't this a beautiful challenge to live *every part* of our lives in authentic ways? We are to be real with others, real with ourselves, and real with God. That about covers everything, right? And done right, we'll be able to find contentment regardless of the imperfections in our relationships because we will see the value in authentic interactions. We'll have the confidence to be who God created us to be— stumbles, fumbles, and all.

But it's not that easy, is it?

The truth is we are broken people living in a broken world trying to navigate our broken lives as we interact with other broken people. In other words, we are all a hot mess. Life doesn't always play fair, and it often leaves us tangled up in fear and unforgiveness and a myriad of insecurities. Does that preach? And we tend to distort authenticity in one of two ways because of that reality:

We can misuse it. We can make authenticity an excuse for our sin.

I have a friend whose husband was cruel to her. I mean, he was downright nasty. He belittled her, saying she needed to lose weight. He criticized her cooking at almost every meal. He was never happy with how she kept the house. And she just couldn't seem to do anything to meet his standards—standards that changed all the time.

A marriage counselor once told him how much his words were hurting his wife. His response was, "I'm just being honest." Well that honesty was misused. It wasn't laced with grace or love or kindness. And because this brand of authenticity was commonplace for him, it eventually cost him his marriage.

Being authentic requires making a judgment call. And quite honestly, not every situation necessitates a painfully frank answer. Sometimes we soften the truth with some compassion. We all have the capacity to speak in kindhearted and generous ways. Now, I'm not advocating that we lie.

I'm just suggesting we don't let our authenticity be used as a weapon. Amen?

You see, when we choose to speak brutal honesty—using our words to purposefully hurt and harm in the name of sincerity—we are misusing authenticity.

We can also misuse it in another way. Some of us have chosen to embrace our immorality and depravity, openly sharing our sinful nature in the name of transparency. Whether it's drinking too much or cussing like a sailor, being sharp-tongued or unabashedly selfish, sometimes we wear our socially acceptable sins like a badge of honor. We say, "It's just how I am" or "It's how I was raised" or "It's because I had a bad childhood," or we make some other excuse to rationalize bad behavior.

Here's the problem. When we do that, we're not asking God to help us be more like Jesus. We're thinking our willingness to be honest about our shortcomings makes us rock stars. We don't take responsibility for our actions and attitudes; rather, we blame our horrible parents, a difficult past, or some other convenient scapegoat. This justification is a misuse of authenticity.

But let's not neglect this truth. Done right, authenticity is beautiful. It's the power of a testimony, and it can give someone strength and resolve to continue fighting for the right outcome. This bad habit of misusing authenticity becomes beneficial when we do two things:

1. Share the truth about the storms we're currently facing (or have faced)
2. Share how God is working in or through the storms to calm the waters (or how we are waiting for Him to intervene)

People need truth, and they also need hope. And when you're a Jesus-girl, the undercurrent of your authenticity is always anchored in the hope of Jesus.

The second way we tend to distort authenticity: *We can refuse it. We can decide to hide who we really are.*

Somewhere along the way we've subscribed to the idea that we should hide our messy, tuck in our crazy, and make it look like we have it all together. Our hearts can't take another hit; we go into self-preservation mode. We may be in the battle of our lives, but no one would know. We hide because we don't want to face criticism, ridicule, or judgment. . .*again.*

Been there, done that, got the T-shirt. Right? If there's anything life has taught us, it's that being vulnerable is risky business. And it can bring pain. So when someone asks how we're doing, we smile and say, "I'm good." Inside, though, we're dying.

But when God made us, He programmed our hearts with the desire to be *known.* We have a built-in hope to be *seen.* And because God created that need in us, it means He also created a way for that need to be met. Sometimes He is the one to do it, but other times it happens through community. His wonderful design included a friend or two to come alongside us as we navigate the ups and downs of life. Think about it:

- Moses had Aaron.
- Jesus had the disciples.
- David had Jonathan.
- Joshua had Caleb.
- Paul had Timothy.

We need people in our lives we can be real with. We need friends who are safe places. And we need women who will come alongside us, affirming our value and significance. This kind of community is at its healthiest when we lower our expectation of its perfection, add a huge dose of grace, and bake in a deep love for Jesus. This is a powerful recipe for authenticity.

But let's dig even deeper and chew on this for a minute. The ability to live authentic is rooted in our belief system. You see, if we believe we're unlovable or unworthy or unacceptable, chances are we'll never feel the freedom to show the world who we really are. We won't risk getting our heart tangled in the knots of insecurity because it will hurt too much. And while family and friends may tell us we're a big bowl of awesomesauce, we don't buy it. The fear of being exposed feels too great and too scary, so we hide and refuse to reveal ourselves. Sound familiar?

If, however, we choose to believe we are who God says we are, authentic living doesn't feel like swimming upstream in a torrential flood. We may struggle with insecurities, but we've anchored our identity in Jesus instead of in the opinions of others. We might be fully aware of our shortcomings, but we know they don't disqualify us from loving and being loved. And so we can open up without fear of rejection or judgment—*at least most of the time.*

Oh yes, at my very core I believe our willingness to open up and be authentic is fully rooted in what we believe about ourselves. And the only way we'll have a healthy self-worth is by being certain that our true identity—how God created us—rests in how God sees us. (We'll cover this big-time in chapter 4, so sit tight.)

Having confidence in that truth helps us navigate each day with conviction. It gives us courage to be real rather than worry about what others think of us. When we trust God's truth about who we are, our authenticity will naturally shine into the world. And that decision to believe God will give us the grit and grace to be honest about what we think and feel.

Even more, authentic living means your eyes are wide open. At the Holy Spirit's prompting, you're able to see when insecurities like shame, guilt, unforgiveness, and worthlessness encourage you to hide. It's a superpower of sorts. God gives us spiritual eyes to recognize what's tangling us up so we can take our knots to Him. And in His graciousness, God removes the lies and replaces them with truth. That divine exchange breeds confidence. And confidence breeds authenticity.

Remember, it takes grit (perseverance) and grace (self-forgiveness) to walk this out, because it's hard to be real in a world that promotes fake. Sometimes we have to hold on to authenticity with all we've got, because if we don't, if we give in or give up, we'll eventually compromise and fall into counterfeit living. Been there. Done that. Like yesterday.

Let's explore just what counterfeit living looks like.

COUNTERFEIT LIVING

When we decide we don't feel comfortable being real, for whatever reason, we naturally default to living a counterfeit life. And I mean *default*. It's automatic. Often undetectable. And for most of us, we don't even realize we're not being authentic.

Choosing to hide our true selves is often a result of

living in a broken world full of sin. We've all been hurt, and we've been trained to build an impenetrable fortress around our hearts so we won't get hurt again. Shame has told us to hide so another reminder of *I'm not good enough* can't find its way into our self-worth. We don't share too much for fear of judgment. We don't put ourselves out there for fear of rejection. And we don't get too close to others because they might confirm our greatest fear that we really are unlovable, unacceptable, or unworthy. We don't want to give anyone the opportunity to see we are not as perfect as we're trying to be.

Yep, counterfeit living is self-protection mode on overdrive.

Girlfriend, I get it. On a deep, personal level, I completely understand. We choose fake living because it feels safer. It *mostly* keeps us from uninvited heartache. It allows us some control, helping us negotiate tricky situations with some ease. We feel *relatively* protected from pain, but we're constantly on the defensive. And at my very core, I believe we opt out of authenticity and into counterfeit living for one or more of these four reasons:

1. We're trying to be who others say we should be.
2. We're believing our own lies about who we really are.
3. We're letting society set our standard for what's acceptable and worthy.
4. We're refusing to believe we are who God says we are.

Being real in today's world is a battle every time we wake up. Gone are the days when everything works out, everyone wants to be your friend, naps are required, and sharing is commonplace. That's called preschool, and we got out of that ages ago. We are all adulting now, and the reality is that authentic living is a hard choice *because it's messy*. But even in the messy and the hard, authenticity is a beautiful pursuit.

I'm part of an online group of women called "Build A Sister Up." As the name suggests, the idea is to literally encourage one another in life and ministry. We're all on the front lines with our faith and trying to juggle family, jobs, speaking, writing, and everything in between. It's the most amazing collective of powerful and compassionate Jesus-girls. But I'll be honest. I almost said no to the invitation to join.

More times than I care to share—probably more times than I can remember—women have been the biggest source of heartache in my life. We can be so catty, can't we? I imagine you're nodding your head right now because chances are you have a similar history.

In some circumstances, women have tried to hurt me on purpose. They chose to lash out, and I was left reeling from their wrath. Other times a mean-spirited, passive-aggressive response caught me off guard. I've also experienced situations where the hurt was completely accidental, or no ill intent was meant, but I chose to pick up an offense anyway. And if I were honest, I'd have to admit I've been the one to cause heartaches plenty of times. Gosh, life is hard.

When I was asked to be a part of this group, then, I kind of freaked out. I thought, *Why would I put myself back into a situation where I'll be a sitting duck?* Can you relate to this kind of thinking? You see, sometimes I'd rather tuck away in my house than talk to people. I'd rather do my own thing than risk another heartache. As women, we can be as mean as the day is long. And being introverted makes my desire to hide seem legit to begin with.

It's almost second nature to walk through life trying to manage potential damage. We may not realize we're living in counterfeit ways, regulating what people know about us. And because we have long memories full of times we've felt rejected and judged, authentic living feels too vulnerable. So we open ourselves just enough to stay connected but not enough to get hurt.

I finally responded to the invitation, telling my friend I'd think about it, I'd pray about it, and I'd get back to her soon. That was Carey-speak for, "Let me find an acceptable excuse for why I'm going to say no." Well, God hounded me about it for days. I couldn't let it go. And for some crazy reason, I found myself hopeful and expectant. And in an odd twist of events, I said yes, quickly followed by, "But I may not be super involved because I'm pretty busy."

Today I am *all in* with this group. It's one of my biggest support systems in this season of life. And because we're choosing to have realistic expectations for one another, it feels easy. We're treating one another with kindness and care, so it feels safe. And I'm feeling the freedom to be authentic about my challenges and victories. I love the deep waters of honesty we're treading together. It's so dadgum refreshing I can barely stand it.

Here are seven ways you can help create a healthy community for authenticity:

1. Keep your thoughts focused on truth rather than writing false stories in your mind.
2. Remember that while you don't have to be perfect, you do have to be purposeful to love others.

3. Find grace for others, releasing them from expectations that aren't fair.
4. Find the grit to stay engaged when you want to hide.
5. Decide that authenticity is worth the risk. . .*again*.
6. Ask God for the courage to be honest about who you are.
7. Forgive the times community has hurt you in the past.

There is no doubt about it—authenticity is risky. But it is worth it. And God will give us the confidence to be who He created us to be so we can make a difference in our communities. He designed us to be authentic voices in the world. And He is asking us to live our lives in genuine ways.

Here's scripture to back that up.

> *Do not allow this world to mold you in its own image. Instead, be transformed from the inside out by renewing your mind. As a result, you will be able to discern what God wills and whatever God finds good, pleasing, and complete. . . .Love others well, and don't hide behind a mask; love authentically.* (Romans 12:2, 9 voice)

In other words, don't let the world tell you who you're supposed to be. Let God remind you of who you already are and choose to stand in that knowledge. When you know your identity is in Christ, it will help you understand and embrace God's will for your life. You'll be able to love with a genuine heart. You'll be able to extend grace and put yourself out there again. And as we've already discovered and will dive into more in chapter 3, our ability to live authentically is rooted in knowing our true identity.

These verses from Romans are a wonderful call to action. You see, authenticity matters to God. And because it matters to Him, it needs to matter to us. We can't decide authenticity is too messy or too hard or too risky and toss in the towel. Well we can, but that conclusion is the opposite of God's plan. It's not the way He wants us to live our one and only life on planet Earth.

This book was written with you in mind, sweet one. At times it will challenge you, push you, affirm you, encourage you, and even walk along with you as you embrace authentic living. From chapter 4 through chapter 12, we're going to use the word *AUTHENTIC* as an acrostic, looking at nine ways to help us find the confidence we need to be ourselves in a world that tells us to be someone else.

I'm giving you permission to be you. Sometimes we just need someone to tell us it's okay. So here it is: *It's okay to be you!* Yes, even with your divine complexities and glorious imperfections, you are good. You are worthy of love. You have so much to offer the world.

Show them who you really are.

Together, let's find the grit and grace to live the authentic life.

CHAPTER 3

It All Starts with Identity

Until you have answered the question "Who am I"
you will not be capable of living your own life.
—Sunday Adelaja[5]

I'm up in the mountains as I write this chapter. It's summer, which means schedules are cray-cray thanks in part to my two teenagers being out of school. Now, I'm one of those moms who loves to hang out with her kids—I love every bit of my time with them—but a point comes when I need to slip away so I can get some adulting done. Thankfully, my husband is always willing to work from home so I can carve out time to write. He's kind of a rock star.

The truth is my creativity flows the very best when I'm in a quiet, uninterrupted space. This is one of those times.

As I rolled out of bed this morning, I threw on a sweatshirt that didn't match my jammie bottoms, grabbed my oversized coffee mug that goes with me everywhere, and shuffled my way to the lobby of the place where I'm staying. It was early enough that I didn't think to check the state of my hair or the possibility of mascara smeared all over my face. Honestly, none of that mattered. I was a woman on a mission, knowing my only hope of writing included a full mug of coffee posthaste.

When I stepped off the elevator, I noticed a woman at the coffee station. I thought, *Okay, Carey, now is the time to find the grit and grace to be human. And kind. I know you can do this.* She had a book in hand by one of my favorite Christian authors, and within minutes we found ourselves diving right into a deep-water discussion. Mind you, this was pre-coffee, with me in mismatched clothes and sporting yesterday's hair and makeup. But this divine appointment was more important than all of that. I was struck by her willingness—right there in the lobby—to share a personal struggle with. . .*me.*

She hung her head, saying, "I just don't know what I'm supposed to do. God isn't telling me anything." This beautiful soul was looking for purpose. She was wondering what gifts she had to offer the world. She was questioning her significance. And she was up early, hoping for some quiet time to explore with the Lord before her family got up.

More than anything, my new friend was confused. Since leaving a lucrative career and unable to financially contribute to the family—something she'd done since forever—she was questioning her value as a wife and mom. Even with a supportive husband, she was having a hard time finding joy and happiness and contentment. She was restless, frustrated by her lack of direction.

This sweet woman was wrestling with her identity. For so many years, she defined herself as a significant financial contributor to the family. It was her main role in the family. And now she wondered, *If I'm not that woman anymore, who am I?*

Can you relate? Sometimes big changes like that are a shock to our systems. What was, isn't anymore. How we've defined ourselves—the interior self—can change too. And it can take time for the reality of those changes to kick in.

Maybe you're divorced and struggling to understand the single you, or just married and learning how to fully welcome another person into your life. Maybe you're a new mom or a new empty nester and aren't sure how life should look now. Or maybe you've been diagnosed with a chronic illness and you're navigating the loss of your health. We let these kinds of things define who we are.

Struggling with identity is a core reason we struggle to live in authentic ways. You see, we can't be *real* unless we know who we *really* are. We must settle some things in our hearts first, because until we understand that our true identities don't change when our life situations change, we won't have the ability to live authentically with ourselves, others, or God. See the rub?

Being married or single. . .having a house full of kids or having no kids at all. . .being healthy or struggling to manage a sickness. . .making six figures or living paycheck to paycheck. . .these kinds of things have nothing to do with your true identity. These are the roles you play, the ways you influence, and the contributions you make to the world. Please, please, please hear my heart, because knowing this next truth nugget is vital to living an authentic life. Here goes:

When your roles and responsibilities, your places of authority, or your ability to make an impact changes, your identity does not. It can't. And because of Jesus, it won't.

I'm going to drop a bunch of scripture in your lap. It's time to hunker down in the Word of God and let His truth wash over us. Gosh, we need to know these promises, especially because it's easy to saturate our hearts in the fakeness of the world. And when we do, we forget that our identity is meant to be anchored in Jesus *alone*.

God's Word is a powerful course corrector. It can snap us back to reality—back to truth. But sometimes we skim scripture or skip it altogether. I'm asking you to engage. Maybe you've grown up with these verses, so they're familiar, or maybe you've heard them taught over and over again, so you're tempted to move on to the next section. Please don't. I'm asking you to focus on them right now. If you do, I'll be your best friend. Deal?

Would you take a minute and ask God for fresh eyes and new revelation? There's so much truth packed into what I'm going to share, and I don't want you to miss a thing. Let these truths sink into the marrow of your weary bones and breathe life into them. Even more, let God solidify your identity—your authentic self.

This next section is all about who you are. It's about who God created you to be. And remember that no matter what, His handiwork in you is unchangeable. This is who *you* are—your true and authentic self. Your identity.

THE BLUEPRINT FOR HUMANITY

At the very beginning of the world, God made man and woman. He didn't come up with a new blueprint. Instead,

He used one already in place.

> Then God said, "Let Us (Father, Son, Holy Spirit) make man in Our image, according to Our likeness [not physical, but a spiritual personality and moral likeness]; and let them have complete authority over the fish of the sea, the birds of the air, the cattle, and over the entire earth, and over everything that creeps and crawls on the earth." So God created man in His own image, in the image and likeness of God He created him; male and female He created them." (Genesis 1:26–27 AMP, emphasis mine)

Did you notice the word *created* was mentioned three times in the last verse? The number three represents completeness. Wholeness. I think it's cool to note that when God created us, it was all-inclusive. We were the last of His creation, the perfect ending to a beautiful process.

Now, being created in His image does not mean we have divinity. It doesn't mean we have a body to reflect His, since He is spirit in nature. But it does mean we are fashioned after Him, being superior to every other creature God made. And even more, we are set apart intellectually, ethically, and socially. We have the unique ability to choose right from wrong, good from bad, and thrive in community.

You see, from the very beginning you were created in His likeness. And because God doesn't make trash, your authentic self holds greatness and importance to your Creator. Trying to be anything or anyone else—trying to conform to who the world says you should be—is a huge left turn from who God made you to be. Sister, your blueprint is nothing short of perfection.

The Blueprint of You

We've acknowledged that God created mankind as a whole in His own image. But in Jeremiah 1:5, it gets a bit more personal. Check this out:

> *"I knew you before you were formed within your mother's womb; before you were born I* sanctified *you and* appointed *you as my spokesman to the world."* (TLB, emphasis mine)

How unbelievably beautiful. Think about this powerful statement for a minute. Before you were even conceived, God knew you. Please read that again. Way back in the day, before the creation of the earth, before the seas were split and animals were formed, God thought *you* up. He *planned* for you before He hung the stars in the sky. He chose every detail of your existence, including the value you would bring into the world. Your authentic self was blueprinted with meticulous delight, order, and purpose.

You were *sanctified* (blessed, approved, dedicated, made holy) and *appointed* (chosen, selected, picked) to bring the Good News of Jesus into the world, even before you took your first gulp of earthly air. This is your authentic self—your true self. This is who you were created to be. It cannot be disputed because God tells us it's fact. And because He is incapable of lying, we have no choice but to believe this to be 100 percent, absolute truth.

What a powerful and impressive reality. I hope you feel the weight of it bearing down on your heart right now—in a good way, of course. If we can absorb this into our *selves,* we will find authentic living to be a much easier task than if we're constantly questioning our existence.

OUR BLUEPRINT FROM GOD'S WORD

Hopefully you've been able to settle these truths in your heart: God created us in His image, and we were blessed and chosen before we were even a twinkle in our mother's eye. But, friend, we are so much more.

Let's look at who God says we are throughout His Word. This list won't be exhaustive, but it will be meaty. Remember, this is not who you *might* become. This isn't who you should *strive* to become. No. This is who you are. *Right now.*

- You are a new creation (2 Corinthians 5:17).
- You are cared for (Philippians 4:19).
- You are forgiven (Ephesians 1:7).
- You are blameless (Ephesians 1:4).
- You are free (Galatians 5:1).
- You are a citizen of heaven (Philippians 3:20).
- You are bold (Ephesians 3:12).
- You are an overcomer (1 Corinthians 10:13).
- You are justified (Romans 5:9).
- You are a child of God (John 1:12).
- You are the light of the world (Matthew 5:14).

This list only scratches the surface. Sweet mother, your identity is so much richer and deeper and wider than what I just shared. I want to encourage you to dig into the Word yourself and write down all that you are because of Jesus. Just google "my identity in Jesus" and you'll be flooded with sites that point you to scripture.

These biblical truths are truths about *you*. These are the foundation of who you are—your authentic self. And if we were both honest, we'd admit that sometimes it takes real grit to believe these things. It takes a flood of grace to think someone like you and me—with our history of bad choices or current season of sinning—could be thought of in these kinds of ways. But we are. And they are unchangeable truths we must choose to believe if we're going to live authentically. There's no way around it.

And although these truths were written long ago, they still apply today. That's one of the most beautiful things about the Bible. The Word of God stays relevant, *never* losing its application and significance. It's alive and active. And if anyone tells you otherwise, they are wrong.

While I love every word of the verses listed above, this passage from 1 Peter 2:9 speaks the loudest into my soul:

> *But you are a chosen people, set aside to be a royal order of priests, a holy nation, God's own; so that you may proclaim the wondrous acts of the One who called you out of inky darkness into shimmering light.* (VOICE)

Friend, you are *chosen*. You have been *set aside*. You are *divine royalty*. You are *God's own*. You have a *voice* and *purpose*. You have been *called*. And you have been *saved* from the darkness and brought into light to shine!

This is a proclamation! And it deserves to be spoken into the world as your own personal "I am" declaration. This is truth you need to hold on to because it defines your authentic self. Let's read this out loud together. Full voice.

Ready? Here we go. . .

I am chosen.
I have been set aside.
I am divine royalty.
I am God's own.
I have a voice and a purpose.
I have been called.
I have been saved.
And I'm here to shine!

Yes and amen, times infinity and beyond. Want to boil down the essence of who you are? Want to know your identity in a nutshell? Well, you just declared it, friend. You just spoke out your authentic self. Boom.

But here's where it gets tricky. The Enemy never wants you to believe it. He knows if you truly believe you are who God says you are, he is in big trouble. If you have the bold confidence to live in authenticity, you're a force to be reckoned with. But all too often we forget who we are because life beats us down and wears us out. Sometimes it's easier to wave the white flag in defeat than stand firm against a barrage of criticism or navigate tangles of insecurity.

A few years ago, police arrested a couple in Arkansas for allegedly starving and beating their four-year-old daughter. They found bruises all over her body. She had one black eye, and the other was swollen. Her forehead was cut, and she had scars across her back. This little girl had dried blood in the corner of her mouth and cord marks on her wrist. Can you even imagine?

The stories of what this couple allegedly did to their daughter are so horrific I won't even share them with you.

But what hit me the hardest was the little girl's response when the police asked for her name. She replied, "My name is idiot." This was her identity based on lies and abuses. That was the name she responded to.

How could something like this have happened? Well, it did, and atrocities like it happen every day. But even when we're told we are who we are not in a much less horrifying manner, the target is our sense of identity with the aim to destroy our confidence.

In those broken moments and seasons of defeat, more than anything else we need reminders of who we are. And honestly, God is the only one who can reignite that truth for us. Friends and family can offer encouragement, but we need our Creator to realign our thoughts with His. And fortunately, He is masterful at it. Let's look at the story of Gideon.

The Israelites were under the harsh oppression of the Midianites. You can read the whole story in Judges 6. They were at the end of their rope, unable to make a life for themselves, and so they cried out to God. In response, He sent an unnamed prophet. Here was his message:

> "I brought you out from slavery in Egypt. I delivered
> you from the Egyptians, from all who would have
> oppressed you. I drove the Canaanites out before you and
> delivered their land into your care. But I said to you,
> 'I am the Eternal One, your True God, and you must
> not worship the gods of the Amorites, those people in
> whose land you settle.' And you have not listened to Me."
> (Judges 6:8–10 VOICE)

The prophet's message is clear and simple. When the Israelites obey God, they are blessed. And when they disobey, He removes His blessing. Every time. And while this isn't news to them, God's people are in a bad spot, feeling discouraged and hopeless.

When we meet Gideon, it doesn't take long to see he wasn't the bravest in the bunch. He was so worried the invaders might steal his grain that he hid inside a winepress to thresh it. Let's just say he wasn't the one people would expect to stand up to oppressors.

But God knew who He made Gideon to be even if Gideon didn't realize it. And when the Lord saw him cowering to the Midianites, He sent a reminder. This was a life-changing moment and message for Gideon. It was an encouragement to embrace his true identity rather than shrink back in fear. God wanted Gideon to see himself the way God had always seen him. Here is how that played out in verses 12 and 14–16 (VOICE, emphasis mine).

> **Messenger of the Eternal One:** *The Eternal One is with you,* mighty warrior. . . .
>
> **Eternal One** (*speaking through His messenger*): *Go out with your strength and rescue Israel from the oppression of Midian. Do you understand that I am the one sending you?*
>
> **Gideon:** *But, Lord, how am I supposed to deliver Israel? My family is the* weakest *in the tribe of Manasseh, and I am the* least *of my family.*
>
> **Eternal One:** *Go. I will be with you, and you will totally destroy the forces of Midian as one man.*

This passage is so revealing, offering us a snapshot of exactly how Gideon saw himself. He was blind to the truth. And while he thought of himself as the *weakest* of the tribe and the *least* in his family, God most certainly did not. He called Gideon a *mighty warrior*. God saw the authentic Gideon—the one He created.

Here's how the story ended. While he struggled to believe he could deliver the Israelites, God continued to affirm Gideon. And eventually Gideon chose to believe God. He stepped out in confidence, followed God's instructions, and liberated his people just like God promised.

Friend, you and I have a choice to make. Like Gideon, we can subscribe to the world's messages—the ones telling us we're the weakest and the least—or we can have confidence in who God says we are. We can entertain our own self-doubt, leaving us to cower in our insecurity, or we can stand in our awesomeness. We can muster the grit and grace it will take to move forward, trusting God to give us what we need to do what He's asking, or we can hide away in fear. It's our choice.

Gideon felt one way, but it wasn't the right way. He allowed his feelings to rule his actions. He let his feelings become his truth. He let how he felt deflate his confidence. But feelings change with the wind, and so will our self-worth if we tie the two together.

Think about it. You may walk out of the salon feeling all sassy with your new hairdo, exuding confidence because your style is trendy and adorable. That is, until no one notices the change. Then you begin to doubt yourself: *I must look foolish. Maybe I'm too old for this kind of hairstyle. Why do I always make bad choices?* And just like that, regardless of the truth, your feelings take over.

Feelings are not always fact. And while we need them to be validated because it does something powerful for our hearts, we also need to know the truth. We can't live in our feelings; we must live in the truth. Sometimes they are one and the same, but most of the time they are not.

You see, standing in the truth is what enables us to live authentic, to live true to how God made us. Let's learn how to combat how we *feel* with what God says is *real*. When a negative feeling presents itself, ask God for truth. Then write it down or speak it aloud. Here's how that might look:

> I may feel *weak*, but God calls me *mighty*.
> I may feel *unlovable*, but God calls me *captivating*.
> I may feel *unacceptable*, but God calls me *treasured*.
> I may feel *insignificant*, but God calls me *valuable*.
> I may feel *rejected*, but God calls me *wanted*.
> I may feel *fake*, but God calls me the *real deal*.
> I may feel ____, but God calls me ____.
> I may feel ____, but God calls me ____.

Make sense? This is an exchange exercise. We're learning to exchange a feeling for a truth. And honestly, I think unbelieving an untruth is one of the hardest things to do. It requires God's strength. But if we ask Him to make the exchange for us, ask Him to transform our minds so we can make choices that align our thoughts with His, He will. And that will give us the ability to live authentic with ourselves, others, and God.

My teenage son has a friend we just love. These two have been through thick and thin together, and they've stood in the gap for each other through some tricky seasons. They'll probably be friends until they see Jesus face-to-face. But just the other day, it got pretty messy.

One of my son's strengths is kindness. He is by far the nicest person in our family. I'm not kidding. He'd give you the shirt off his back. But be careful. Chances are it will smell like a teenage boy, and that's not always super pleasant.

But I digress.

Piloting relationships with kindness is one of the ways Sam lives authentic. It's a God-given strength. But sometimes he misuses that kindness by choosing to keep the peace rather than speak the truth. He'll push down his frustration instead of advocate for himself. He'll stay quiet and let the actions of others aggravate and annoy him. Rather than deal with exasperation when it comes up, he bottles it up. And rather than risk hurting someone's feelings, he sometimes lets others walk all over him. It's a beautiful strength misused.

As my husband and I walk him through tough situations—reminding him that the way he's feeling isn't necessarily the truth of a friendship—we encourage him to be honest with himself and his friend. Gosh, that's a tightrope even the most seasoned adult would struggle to walk. I know from experience. But to live authentic, we must muster the grit to be open and honest and the grace to be compassionate and caring.

As we try to live real, rarely does grit or grace come without the other. It really does take both to live authentic. It really does matter that we seek truth over feelings. But it all starts with identity, friend. My hope is that you have a clearer picture of who you are, how you were created, and the value in knowing those truths. We simply cannot live genuine lives unless we genuinely know ourselves.

But how do we walk that out? What are some practical

ways we can be authentic in our everyday lives? How can we thrive in authentic community? Good questions! And if you've read either of my previous books, you know I'll never offer head knowledge without also giving you marching orders. Sometimes we just need someone to tell us what to do or how to do it. And that's what this book is all about.

Listen, when we really sink our teeth into the truth that our identity is fully rooted in our Creator, it will change everything. We'll be stronger in our resolve to be real. We'll be unshakable in the convictions of who we are. . .and who we are not. We'll be faster to reject the untruths that bombard our hearts. And we'll walk in a new level of peace and confidence.

Gosh, who wouldn't want that?

In the next nine chapters, we're going to unpack the nine ways we can live authentic lives with ourselves, others, and God. I'm so proud of you for choosing to do this kind of heart work. God will bless you for digging into this with Him. Good job!

Now, stay focused. Stay present. Stay engaged. And remember I'm right here with you, praying for God to wreck your heart with the reality of your awesomeness. I'm asking Him to ignite your passion for authenticity. I'm asking for a desire to pursue truth over feeling. And I'm trusting that God will solidify your identity in Him above all else.

Let's do this. Together.

CHAPTER 4

Accept Your Awesomeness

Wanting to be someone else is a waste of the person you are.
—Marilyn Monroe[6]

The words above from Marilyn Monroe are pretty powerful—especially coming from a woman who probably lived with a great deal of regret. Maybe these words spilled out of deep places because she understood them on a personal level. She wanted fame and allowed the industry to change her into someone else. Norma Jean gave way to Marilyn, and she eventually lost her life to a barbiturate overdose that might have been intentional.

I don't pretend to know the ins and outs of this beautifully broken woman, nor do I have insight into all the reasons her life came to such an end at the age of thirty-six. But when I read this quote from her, I hear regret. I hear remorse. I hear a woman who wishes for a do-over. And it gets my attention.

From the grave, Marilyn is warning us not to waste our

lives wishing we were different. Or better. Yet many of us spend most of our time here on earth looking around at everyone else, wishing we *could* be like them. We want their marriages. Their finances. Their kids. Their travel itineraries. Their bodies or skin or hair. We want their fame. Their careers. And it is creating discontentment in epic proportions.

I love me some long eyelashes. When I was younger, mine were decent. But nowadays, I have to work it to get any kind of length at all. I hate it. So on my fortieth birthday, I bought myself a trip to the salon for lash extensions. I lay on the table as someone spent the next hour or so adding lashes to my natural ones. Inside I was giddy, like a child waiting in line for the merry-go-round. I can't even find the right words. My heart was packed full of hope, certain that luscious eyelashes held the power to make me feel better about *me*.

Two hours after those beautiful lashes were glued to my lid, the allergic reaction started. My eyes began to swell and turn red. They burned and watered. And after riding it out for the rest of the day, praying my angry eyes would settle down, I went back to the salon and had them taken off. Ugh. I was so discouraged and frustrated. Oh, and happy stinkin' birthday to me.

Jump ahead ten years to now. Just a few weeks ago, a makeup artist put a temporary set of eyelashes on me for a video shoot. More than anything that happened that day, I was the most excited for the long lashes. Before the day even started, she knew these were at the top of my makeup to-do list. Seriously. Even typing this makes me giggle. It's the simple things, friends! What is it about eyelashes that make a woman feel more beautiful?

As she was fitting them to my eyelids, she told me they might last into the next day but not much longer. And she was right. Here's the funny (and slightly pathetic) part. Even with sections coming unglued and hanging a little wonky in places, I kept those puppies on for two more days. I kid you not. I thought, *A girl's gotta do what a girl's gotta do.*

In the end, here was the question I had to ask myself: *What is wrong with my own lashes to begin with?* Okay, sure, they lack lusciousness. In my natural state, I don't have as many to work with as I used to. But long lashes don't make me a better person. I'm not more lovable because of them. The lashes won't make me smarter or richer or braver. The answer to my question was simple. There's nothing wrong with my lashes. *The problem was with me.*

With misguided reasons, many of us have decided that who we are is not good enough. We're afraid of falling short. We're too busy craning our necks from left to right, checking out everyone else. In our minds, the image in the mirror isn't what it should be—not by a mile.

Think about this and be honest. When you look at your reflection, how many angles do you check out before you decide on your outfit for the day? And in that same vein, how many outfits do you try on before settling? When you're checking yourself out, what woman comes to mind? In other words, who is the standard you're trying to measure up to?

You see, in too many areas we're falling prey to an *us* against *them* mentality. We're looking critically at parts of our bodies or parts of our lives, and we're hating what we see. Often without even realizing it, we're creating measuring sticks and using them to confirm what we already feel— that we're not *acceptable.* And so rather than be happy for her or them, we secretly despise the thing we envy the most. We just can't see that our authentic self is full of its own unique awesomeness.

It's an endless cycle, and it's exhausting.

While I loved those fake lashes because they made me feel womanlier, the truth is I wanted others to notice them. I wanted my husband to find me irresistible. I wanted my friends to think I looked years younger. And I wanted strangers to envy them, wishing theirs were the same. *Did I really just admit that?*

Can we be real for a minute? Sometimes it feels good when others envy us. We spend so much of our time being envious that just knowing someone envies *us* makes it seem more normal. It makes the comparison trap more acceptable. And when we think others find us cooler than they are, our self-worth inflates. There's a whole lot of unhealthy going on with this, but one thing stands out the most. Think about it. Why do we feel better about ourselves when someone is envious of what we have or are? Why is being accepted by others a prerequisite to us accepting ourselves? Why can't we accept our own brand of awesome?

I know. I just stepped on your toes. Does it help knowing I just stepped on my own toes? That last paragraph was a doozy to write with truth hard to hear. But we need to understand this toxic tendency to want—*to need*—the approval of others. We must see the dysfunction in thinking we're lovable only if others think we are. Unless we recognize it, these untruths will fester, and we'll continue entertaining these kinds of deadly lies in our hearts. And even more, this unhealthy cycle won't be brought into alignment with God's truth about who we really are.

Do you remember our conversation from the last chapter about 1 Peter 2:9? That scripture solidified the authentic self as one chosen, set aside, divinely royal, God's own, saved, and called. I'm praying our discussion already settled this truth in your heart, because these things are what make you fully accepted and approved of right here and now. I know it takes both grit and grace to believe it, and I'm hoping you do. And I also hope you noted that nothing in that list from 1 Peter depends on the thoughts or opinions of others.

Here's how that looks in real life.

Think of a time you bought a new outfit, something different from the style you normally wore. It felt a little risky, but you were feeling confident. Then when your husband saw you wearing it for the first time, he squished his face and shook his head. He made it obvious your new duds were a no-go. Somehow his reaction stole the excitement and left you feeling ugly. And this can happen with a relative or friend too.

Or maybe you said yes and tried something new. It felt a bit scary, but you put in the time and effort and thought you shined. Your confidence was at an all-time high. But when you asked someone for feedback—expecting a job-well-done response—they pointed out where you fell short. And you felt shame.

Maybe you tried hard to fit into that group of women you admire. You reached out to each one individually, trying to find a connecting point. And just when you felt as if your efforts were working and friendships were forming, you saw the Instagram picture of a girls' night out—one to which you weren't invited. You were left feeling hurt, unseen, and unwanted.

Why are we investing so much of our hearts in what others think? The problem is that we're letting their opinions become our gauge of goodness. We're letting their comments become the measuring sticks for our self-worth. Even if twenty people tell us we're amazing, we obsess over the one who didn't. And worse, even when God tells us we're awesome, we don't believe Him.

I remember stepping off a stage one time, feeling so good about the message I had just delivered. I was pumped, and I felt God's delight for stepping out in obedience. But when I asked a friend for her opinion—a sad attempt for validation—she shrugged her shoulders and said, "I think you went a little long. You were good, but I think you could have summed it up a bit faster."

My heart seemed to drop to the floor as her response knocked the wind out of me. I felt exposed and embarrassed (that's shame, by the way). It didn't matter that God found my words pleasing and honoring; I felt ridiculous. And even though that was years ago, that message from my friend hits repeat after almost every speaking engagement. It leaves me wondering if what I just did on stage was acceptable.

As women, we crave validation. Gosh, I don't know a woman out there who doesn't want to know she's a big bowl of awesomesauce. Some may need it more than others, but every single one of us wants to know we're okay, we're lovable, and we're acceptable. Dagnabit, girls, it's just human nature to want affirmation from others.

So can we all raise our hands and admit we have a validation problem? Can we agree we all need to muster some grit and grace so we can believe that God finds us 100 percent acceptable? It's refreshing to have an honest conversation, knowing we all struggle. We're all in this together. Let's step down from the judgment seat and link arms as women.

Truth be told, our craving for acceptance isn't only natural; it's also placed there by God Himself—*on purpose*. I believe He put in each of us a fierce desire to belong. We want to know we fit into the world, that we matter and are significant. I also believe God planned all along to meet that need in remarkable ways.

Let this sink in, sweet one. When you were created, God thought through every single detail. He knew the perfect gifts and talents to bake into you. He chose the perfect set of life experiences—both challenges and joys—you'd encounter. He decided your family, your friends, and what other community groups you'd be connected to. God even chose the perfect time to bring you onto the Kingdom calendar. You're not a mistake or an orphan. You were planned from the very beginning.

The most amazing part of our design is that God created us in His own image. That means right from the start, we've been 100 percent accepted by the One who made the heavens and the earth—and everything in them. We don't need to add anything to make ourselves more pleasing to God. From the beginning, we've had His stamp of approval. But somewhere along the way, you and I have decided to unbelieve this truth. And it's gotten us into trouble.

We've essentially chosen to ignore what *God knows* about us and opted for what *humanity thinks* of us. No wonder we're a mess. I don't know about you, but I'm tired of living this way. I want to find the grit and grace to accept my awesomeness without being afraid to be who God created me to be. I want to find the confidence to live my one and only life in authentic ways. And more than anything, I want the courage to believe God about who I really am.

In the book of Mark, we read about a father desperate for Jesus to heal his son. From birth, this child has been possessed, and the father doesn't want to accept this condition as his son's future. For those of you who are parents, don't you know how much he wants healing for his child? Can't you imagine his hopes for a normal life for his boy? The dad doesn't want to settle for his son being less than who he was created to be. And in that moment of desperation, the Messiah asks for the boy to be brought to Him.

This is the exchange in Mark 9:22–24 (VOICE, emphasis mine):

> **Father:** *I have run out of options; I have tried everything. But if there's anything You can do, please, have pity on us and help us.*
>
> **Jesus:** *What do you mean, "If there's anything?" All things are possible, if you only believe.*
>
> **Father** *(crying in desperation): I believe, Lord. Help me to believe!*

Everything in this man wanted to believe. He wanted to let go of the *if* and cling to the *all*. And rather than sit in his unbelief, he found some grit. He knew his son was valuable and had purpose, and rather than settle, he begged Jesus for help.

What if we asked God for the same thing? When we struggle believing the truth that we're acceptable—when we feel undesirable, when we think we're unwanted—what if we found the grit to pray, *God, help me with my doubt!* Oh, I think it would be beautiful

Once the demon left the boy, verse 27 tells us, "Jesus took the boy by the hand and lifted him to his feet" (VOICE). In His power, Jesus removed the oppressive spirit and restored this child to his true self—his authentic self. He helped him find his footing again. In that miraculous moment, Jesus removed the label of unacceptable placed on him by his community and possibly even himself. Jesus gave him his life back.

That's what the Lord offers us. In all His glory and power, He does whatever it takes to remind us of who we are. He reminds us we're acceptable no matter what—and we always have been. As with this young boy, sometimes He does this in ways the entire community can see. Other times he exchanges a lie for truth deep within our heart.

May I share one more powerful passage of scripture with you about our struggle with unbelief, another slam-dunk confirmation that God sees our immeasurable value even when we can't? Let's absorb the words of Jesus.

> "*I am the Bread of Life.* The person who aligns with me hungers no more and thirsts no more, ever. *I have told you this explicitly because even though you have seen me in action, you don't really believe me. Every person the Father gives me eventually comes running to me.* And once that person is with me, I hold on and don't let go." (John 6:35–37 MSG, emphasis mine)

Okay, before we delve more into unbelief, back up the bus. Let that sink in. There's *nothing* we can do to become unacceptable to God.

- Not your bad choice with that guy
- Not the item you stole from a store
- Not the mean way you treated a friend
- Not the string of cuss words you spewed at a driver
- Not the way you lashed out at your kids or husband
- Not the blind eye you turned in that situation

Nothing. This passage is a beautiful reminder that we're always pleasing to Him—*fully and completely*.

This passage also confirms (again) that unbelief is a real thing. Even though some had watched Jesus in action, they *still struggled to believe*. Jesus is basically saying this: "I am everything you need, and I've backed that truth up with my actions. You've witnessed my divine abilities more than once, and yet you still don't believe me." Can we just admit we have a problem with unbelief? Yep, our humanness gets in the way once again.

But it's in the second half of this passage where He becomes so tender (not that He wasn't before) and reminds us that even though we struggle to accept Him—to believe Him—He never struggles to accept us. We are 100 percent acceptable and necessary in the eyes of our heavenly Father. Jesus speaks with great clarity when He tells us we're wholly embraced by Him, and nothing will change that. He says, "I hold on and don't let go."

Let's think through this. I don't really like to hang out with people I don't like. That may sound judgmental, but I wonder if you'd admit the same. I know God calls us to love the unlovable, but I think healthy boundaries are crucial in some situations and with some people. Amen? Life is too short to surround yourself with those toxic to your heart, and that's exactly why I struggle to include them in my tribe.

But here's the thing. *God never struggles.* He loves and accepts me even when I'm snarky, mean-spirited, and hateful. When I use choice words with drivers, He accepts me. When I'm dismissive and rude to my husband or angry and condescending to my kids, I am accepted by my Father. While I might struggle to feel acceptable, at the end of the day God never struggles to accept me. He sees my authentic self, not the set of bad choices I just made.

God sees our worth because He made us. He knows the awesomeness built right into us. And at some point we must find the grit and grace to trust God's words as undeniable proof that we're worthy. It's time we learn to love who He made us to be.

When my daughter went into high school, we transferred her from a Christian private school to a public high school. She needed a fresh start after a tough year riddled with messages that she wasn't enough. I've never seen her struggle so much with friendships. Sweet mother, what that does to a mom's heart.

I can recall several Friday nights when her group of friends (I use the term *friends* loosely) would have a huge sleepover and send pictures from it directly to her. She'd also see the images all over their social media accounts, and it left my daughter feeling unwanted and heartbroken.

Earlier on those days, they'd all sat together at lunch and laughed. She'd walked with them to their next classes, and they texted each other regularly, so every party she wasn't invited to always caught us off guard. Her question was always, "What is wrong with me?" But that mind-set didn't last for long.

My daughter is pretty amazing and chose take the high road—every stinkin' time. These other girls would see her on Monday and make some lame excuse as to why they left her off the party invite. And my baby would smile and extend grace. She wasn't going to let something like that take her down. She found the grit and grace to be herself regardless of the hurtful messages hurling her way.

I, on the other hand, did not take the high road. Moms, do you feel me? I may have looked calm and collected on the outside, but I thought up the cruelest revenge on the inside. Of course, I didn't act it out. I would never survive jail. I need lots of mascara and good coffee, and I'm certain those aren't as readily available for the incarcerated as I'd need them to be. I'm serious.

At her eighth-grade celebration at the end of the year, one of my daughter's teachers pulled me aside. She said, "Carey, Sara is a rare gem. She's courageous and a powerful leader, and I am so sad this group of girls refused to embrace that in her. They've missed out. What I love is that Sara is so confident in who she is. She may get knocked down, but she doesn't stay down. That kid knows who she is in Jesus."

I want to be just like my daughter when I grow up. Maybe you do too. She was unafraid to be herself even though she was underloved and underappreciated. It didn't matter; she loved who God made her to be. And you know what, her confident beauty shined through the hateful plans of those girls.

Sister, you may feel unacceptable. You might have been told you're not up to standard. You might get mixed messages from others, saying you're tolerable at best. You may feel cast aside, unseen, and unloved. And while the pain is real (and I really am sorry), these feelings are not your truth. They don't have the power to define who you truly are, because God has already done that. No, they're absolutely *not* the truth.

May I bring in a reality check? Think about this. The God who created the heavens and the earth, the One who separated the water from the land, the One who set life into motion, the One who allowed His Son to bridge the gap of sin, thought you up and finds you simply irresistible and fully acceptable. And as we've learned, nothing can change that.

It's not dependent on how you perform, how you live or love, what you look like, or your credentials. And you can do nothing to make God love you more or less than He does right now. Remember, you are 100 percent acceptable to the most powerful being in the universe. In His eyes, you are worth Jesus.

So how do we let that truth sink into the marrow of our bones? How does His truth become part of our DNA, help us accept our awesomeness and live with authenticity? Maybe this is a good place to start.

Recognize the Fickleness of Others

In this world, we're going to get mixed messages about our worth just like my daughter did. Others might say we matter, but their actions won't line up. They may treat us like one of the gang but talk behind our backs. We might be accepted into the group until the queen bee decides we're unworthy. We might fit "in" for a season and then be "out" without warning. The world is so fickle (including you and me), and it changes its mind so quickly.

We can't let this fickleness affect the truth of who we

are. Engage your grit today so you'll know that truth from this point forward. The ebb and flow of others' opinions doesn't get voting rights for our awesomeness. We cannot be afraid of the world's rejection, because at some point it's inevitable. People are nitpicky and inconsistent, and settling this in our hearts now will help us navigate it with confidence later.

Come on, girls. Let's not give anyone that kind of power—the kind that tells us how we should feel about ourselves. Let's not be so desperate to belong that we try to change who we are.

I love this quote from Brené Brown: "Because true belonging only happens when we present our authentic, imperfect selves to the world, our sense of belonging can never be greater than our level of self-acceptance."[7]

In other words, if you want to experience genuine belonging, *be yourself*. No matter what the world thinks, *be yourself*. Even more, choose to love the whole you even with your divine complexities and glorious imperfections. No one is perfect.

RECOGNIZE THE TENDERNESS OF GOD

Depending on your experiences, this might seem unlikely to you. But all along, from the moment of your birth to this very moment, God has been sending you reminders of your acceptability. From that kind word to that proud moment. . .from that acknowledgment to that promotion . . .from that amazing friend to that loving husband. . .from that breakthrough to that glimpse of God in your mess. . . He has strategically placed tender reminders in your path. Have you seen them?

Well the Enemy has, and he's been trying to cover them up with discouragement and offense ever since. So many times, we've taken the bait. We've said things like, "Does God even care? Where is God? How could He let all these things happen?" Sound familiar?

Instead of believing we're fully accepted and completely loved, we've listened to the Enemy. It's kept us in an endless cycle of believing lies—lies like we're unwanted, outcasts, and insignificant. And every time we question our awesomeness, the Enemy pats his back for a job well done. His goal is to sink rejection deep into our self-worth. He wants to remove the grit and grace we've mustered so we're left questioning our value. Is it working?

Let me speak truth into your weary soul, sister. This is not how God wanted this to go down. Remember, He's been faithful to send consistent and persistent messages of value to you. I know, I know, some of you may be shaking your heads and saying, "How can that even be true? Do you even know my life?" And while I don't, I do know mine.

Let's just say I've not lived a charmed life—not by a mile. It's been marked by abuses of all kinds, divorce, stalking, bad choices, self-hatred, suicidal thoughts, depression, and a cancer diagnosis. These have all left scars of one kind or another, in one way or another. And if I've been able to claw my way to the truth, you can too. If God's been trying to get my attention, I guarantee He's speaking to you as well.

Ask God to open your ears to hear His still, small voice. Ask for spiritual eyes to see His tenderness in your life. And ask for powerful reminders of your awesomeness so you can be confident in who God made you to be.

In chapter 3, we looked at scripture that spoke to our

identity. Let's add to our arsenal. We can never have too much truth to combat the Enemy's lies. The Word of God is clear about who we are and how much God loves us. And I appreciate how He shoots straight with us. There's no mincing of words.

When we're struggling the most, we find the grit and grace to be real in the pages of this Book. It's where we find confidence to overcome the fear that often accompanies authentic living. And sometimes I like to stand in my bedroom and speak these truths out loud. It's empowering, and it makes the Enemy shake in his boots. Feel free to do that right now.

- I am beloved (Colossians 3:12).
- I am able (John 15:5).
- I am full of purpose (Ephesians 2:10).
- I have been justified (Romans 5:1).
- I am forgiven (1 John 2:12).
- I am anointed (1 John 2:27).
- I am loved (1 John 4:10).
- I am complete in Christ (Colossians 2:10).
- I am redeemed (Revelation 5:9).
- I am clean (John 15:3).
- I am free from condemnation (Romans 8:1).
- I am called (1 Corinthians 7:17).
- I am righteous (2 Corinthians 5:21).
- I am blessed with every spiritual blessing (Ephesians 1:3).
- I am God's workmanship (Ephesians 2:10).
- I have direct access to God (Ephesians 2:18).
- I am capable (Philippians 4:13).
- I am victorious through Jesus Christ (1 Corinthians 15:57).

These verses are hard-core proof that God has a tender place in His heart for you. And when I read them or speak them aloud, the hard places in my heart that refuse to see the truth of me soften. I tear up knowing I matter so much to Him. And it makes me realize that I *am* okay—just the way He made me.

Recognize the Choices before You

Sweet friend, the world has taken so much from you—your confidence, your self-image, your sense of belonging, your freedom to be you, your ability to trust, your peaceful heart. I'm encouraging you to take it back. This is your challenge to choose to change things up, once and for all.

When you boil it all down, here are your two choices: believe what the Enemy says about you or believe who God says you are. One choice will leave you striving to be accepted, running on the proverbial treadmill to keep up with the world's standards so you fit in. The other choice will usher in peace.

One of these choices will make you look at yourself with critical eyes and believe what you see. The other one will offer rest and reassurance that you were created on purpose and for a purpose.

One choice will cause you to replay your failures and shortcomings on a loop, being constantly reminded of all the things you are not. The other will remind you of forgiveness and do-overs and grace.

You have a choice.

And one of the best gifts we can give to those around us is an example of a confident woman. Let's show others what accepting our awesomeness looks like. And as we begin this journey to live authentic lives, let's make peace with ourselves. We don't need anyone's permission or validation, because we already have God's.

FINDING THE GRIT

At the beginning of the chapter, we talked about envy. What did you take away from that discussion?

Sometimes we have this toxic tendency to need the approval of others before we can accept ourselves. What does this look like in your life?

Where and why do you crave validation?

What are your thoughts about the father's struggle with unbelief in Mark 9:22–24? How can you relate?

How does accepting your awesomeness affect your ability to live authentic?

FINDING THE GRACE

Father, thank You for Your Word. It speaks to some broken places inside that need reminders of how much You value me. I don't want to be the kind of woman who ignores Your truth and embraces the world's lies instead. I believe; please help my unbelief! I confess that I get tangled in comparison and envy, and I'm asking that You help me love who You made me. Give me courage to be a real deal. Teach me how to find contentment so I can live authentic with myself, others, and You. In Jesus' mighty name, amen

Live
Accept Your Awesomeness
U
T
H
E
N
T
I
C

CHAPTER 5

Unearth the Untruths

If you do not tell the truth about yourself
you cannot tell it about other people.
—Virginia Woolf [8]

For months I had been her rock through some hard situations. We talked every day—three or four times—as she poured out her hurt and pain. It wasn't just one mess; it was several. And they were all colliding at the same time.

My heart was tendered toward my friend. In that season, her life was so big and the pain was so real that it was almost unbearable. And as we processed and prayed daily, we watched the storms begin to calm. She wasn't living at defcon 4 anymore. But then everything changed.

I remember that day so clearly. It was my turn to be messy. Someone's response made me so mad, and I called my friend to vent. When she didn't answer, I left a voice mail explaining my anger toward this person. I let my raw emotions spill out, unfiltered. My words were unkind and unmeasured.

And I was waiting for a call back so she could process what had happened with me—just like I'd done with her for the past several months. But the call didn't come.

Two days later, I reached out via text message. Is EVERY-THING OKAY? DID YOU GET MY MESSAGE? Her text response caught me off guard. YES, I'VE JUST BEEN SUPER BUSY. TALK TO YOU SOON. Too busy. Ouch.

The lies came barreling at me going ninety miles an hour.

You don't have any friends.

You're not worth anyone's time.

You're too messy.

You deserve bad things.

If I had a dime for every untruth I've believed in my fifty-plus years on earth, I'd be a millionaire by now. Twelve times over. I'm totally serious. I've taken the bait more times than I care to count. And it's messed me up in the worst of ways.

It's robbed me of joy and happiness, thinking I didn't deserve either. It's stirred up fear that I'll never be enough or that I'm always too much. Lies have led to bad choices and reckless decisions. They've tangled my heart with in-securities, whispering that approval was conditional and I needed to work for love. And it's made it almost impossible to be real—to be the authentic me—with others. Honestly, I didn't want to be rejected again. I didn't want to risk betrayal. And so I justified hiding my true self from almost everyone. Somehow it just felt safer.

Not only have I believed these lies, but I've given them authority in my life. They've ruled over me, infiltrating my heart and mind. Even as I sit here today, I'm battling lies that are so loud. They scare me because they rock my foundation and make me feel vulnerable. Maybe you know exactly what I'm talking about. And while I don't know what your lies say to you, every lie I've believed has come from the same root belief: *I am too much or not enough.*

When I reached out to my friend from that raw place and left the unfiltered voice mail on her phone, the lack of response said one thing to me: *You're too much.* And without even realizing it, I agreed with the untruth. Again. And it reinforced the belief that "messy Carey" should stay hidden because others don't know what to do with her. I tucked messy me back in and went about my day. I hate that lie. It hurts. And honestly, I'm so tired of believing it.

Lies don't only torment your mind; they affect how you respond to life. They work on your whole person. You see, every time we hear an untruth and agree with it, our behavior patterns change. For example, when the *I'm too much* lie landed on me because my friend didn't return my call, I started acting different. I withdrew, holding on to my hurt rather than processing it with someone safe. I got quiet, afraid someone would tell me I was being too dramatic. And while I was smiling on the outside, a war was being waged on the inside.

I stopped being the authentic me and tried to be someone else—someone more acceptable.

What about you? Let's unearth your untruths. Think through your life. Can you identify lies you may be believing right now? They are usually born out of pain, so maybe think back to the last hurtful situation and ask God to reveal the lie it produced or reinforced. Did someone yell at you? Did you get left out, or did someone walk out? Did a friend or family member make you feel guilty about something you did or ashamed because of who you are? Where do you feel not enough or too much? Where do you feel unworthy, unacceptable, or unlovable?

Write them out here. *I'm believing lies that tell me I am:*

_____

_____

_____

_____

_____

_____

_____

_____

_____

_____

We must see the lies and uproot them. Any untruths that stay deep in the soil of our lives will tangle us. I know discovery isn't much fun. It takes grit and grace to dig in there. But it's good. And unless we sit down and take inventory, the lies will continue to operate unmonitored. We won't realize they are destroying our ability to be authentic.

This is where we stand up and fight back. This is where we have to go to battle against the Enemy so those lies are silenced. I know that might sound scary, but you have authority in Jesus to command the Enemy to leave. When the untruths are overwhelming, I do two things:

1. I ask for the mind of Christ.

In one translation, 1 Corinthians 2:16 says, "But we have the mind of Christ" (NIV). That means we understand God's plan for humanity, we recognize His purposes for us, and we agree with His view on how we should live. As a believer, you have this knowledge available to you.

This chapter is packed with some amazing truths about the mind of Christ. Let me share a few with you:

- Our wisdom is no match for the mind of Christ (vv. 5–6).
- We access and understand the mind of Christ through the Holy Spirit (vv. 10–14).
- We are given discernment in matters that are spiritual (vv. 14–15).

When my mind starts believing untruths, I will literally pray this over and over and over until the crazy stops: *Father, give me the mind of Christ.* And it calms me down every time.

2. I command the Enemy to leave.

Because we know the Enemy is the father of lies (John 8:44), every untruth you are believing comes from him. But *you* have the authority to command the Enemy to leave you alone. There is no reason to cower in fear. Muster the grit to cast him out of your way.

Here is why you can do this:

[Jesus said,] *"I've given you true authority. You can smash vipers and scorpions under your feet. You can walk all over the power of the enemy. You can't be harmed"* (Luke 10:19 voice).

Here is what you say:

In the name of Jesus, I command you to leave me alone.

God has given me authority in His name, and I cast you
back to where you came from. You have no power over
me and must leave right now.

And because you commanded this in Jesus' name, the Enemy must obey. Remember to say it out loud. He cannot read your mind (1 Kings 8:39 says only God knows the human heart).

From the beginning of time, God's plan was for you and me to live authentic lives—the ones He created us to live. God wants us to muster the grit and grace to shine our true selves into the world, glorifying Him. He put something beautiful in each of us we're meant to share with others. And when we hide in fear—overwhelmed by lies—everyone misses out on what we have to offer.

Let's keep this in perspective. Believing lies is inevitable. As I said before, we're broken women living in a broken world, trying to do life with other broken people. There's zero chance we'll escape this world without bumps and bruises along the way. But it's what we do with those lies that makes all the difference.

WHEN WE BELIEVE THE LIES WE SAY TO OURSELVES

Sometimes the truth feels too scary or too big, so we create lies as a coping mechanism to handle the situation. Your marriage might be on the rocks, but you tell yourself everything's fine and keep the status quo. Your body might be sending warning signals that something's wrong, but you chalk it up to being tired. Your finances may be in a downward spiral, but you want to believe it will all work out in the end and don't change your spending habits. Many of us cover up our reality with lies that make us feel better.

When we do this, we're living in denial. I can think of many times I've chosen to ignore reality because it scared me. I thought if I ignored it and focused on how I wanted things to be, it would happen. Kind of the "fake it till you make it" mentality. The problem is it doesn't always work out that way. Sometimes it's so easy—almost a reflex—to turn a blind eye to the facts and create a more palatable scenario.

But when we decide to operate in an alternative universe, we're not being authentic with ourselves. We're ignoring the power of God in our lives. And we're teaching the next generation to do the same.

I had a friend once who struggled with her tweener daughter's attitude. Her biggest complaint was that the girl played the victim and never owned her part in messy situations. Their relationship was tenuous at best, and she blamed her husband's genes for this "character flaw" in their daughter. The funny thing is, that tweener is just like her mother. The apple didn't fall far from the tree. But my girlfriend never saw it, and when I mentioned it she laughed it off.

It felt better to blame her husband's genetic influence than take a good hard look at herself. And while I honestly think deep down she knew her daughter was taking her lead, she just didn't want to own it.

Hey, I get it. Sometimes I get tired of playing adult too. But unfortunately and thankfully, part of being authentic means we man up (woman up) and see the truth for what it is rather than turning a blind eye and hoping for the best. We stop hiding behind the lies we've created for ourselves and embrace the truth, even if that's a little messy and ugly.

On the other side of the spectrum, many of us use untruths to beat up ourselves. We become our own worst critics. We don't ignore the lies; we use them as ammunition. And our self-worth is the victim.

A friend invited me to take part in a twenty-four-hour challenge designed to uncover the lies I say to myself every day. Because I was pretty sure nothing would be found, I agreed to it. But oh my, so many untruths were unearthed. I wasn't being real with myself. I was filling my heart with hurtful lies.

> *My wrinkles make me look old and ugly.*
> *Why do people tag me on Facebook? I hate the way I look.*
> *My hair is nowhere as cute as hers.*
> *She is always the one to connect with me first. She's such a better friend.*
> *I haven't called my sister in weeks. I'm so lame.*
> *Where are my car keys? I'm so stupid not to hang them up by the door when I come in.*

This kind of internal dialogue leaves me feeling wretched about myself. It makes me feel like I should work harder. It tells me who I am is not okay. And that's not okay with God.

Remember, according to 1 Peter 4:9, you are *chosen*. You have been *set aside*. You are *divine royalty*. You are *God's own*. You have a *voice* and *purpose*. You have been *called*. And you have been *saved* from the darkness and brought into light to shine! We have no grounds for name calling because God says you were created on purpose.

Why don't you take the same challenge?

For the next twenty-four hours, write down all the mean-spirited and hurtful things you say to yourself. This is just another opportunity to unearth the untruths keeping you from living authentic.

Listen, friend, we are partnering with self-condemnation on epic levels, and it has to stop. We don't need others to tell us we're too much or too little; we're doing it to ourselves in spades. And those lies are affecting our self-worth, encouraging us to hide our true selves.

Anytime we pull untruths out of the dark and into the light, they lose their grip on us. Because that's where healing is. That's where freedom comes in. It's what allows us to live in authentic ways, being who God created us to be.

WHEN WE BELIEVE THAT GOD LIES TO US

I hated typing the heading above. I even tried to find another way to say it, but in all honesty, I think it's accurate. Let's dig in.

God and truth go hand in hand. There's no way to disconnect the two from each other. Just like chips and salsa, peanut butter and jelly, and me and coffee, God and truth are inseparable. You can't have one without the other. And we get into big trouble when we think differently.

Would you agree that sometimes we have selective hearing and selective believing? Think about it. We may hear someone tell us God is good, but we only sort of believe it. We may think He is good to only certain people. Or we think we'll earn His favor if we're "good" Christian girls (whatever that means). We may even think our past disqualifies us from His goodness, believing God's love is conditional.

This kind of thinking may be *our* truth, but that doesn't make it true. When we think God is anything other than who He says He is in the Bible, we're calling Him a liar.

And, friend, when we think we're anything other than who God says we are in the Bible, we're denying our authentic self. Plain and simple.

As Jesus-girls, we must make a choice. Either we're going to believe everything God says or nothing at all. We have to trust the Bible in its entirety or decide it's flawed. We embrace all of Jesus' teachings or think they're just cute stories. It's all or nothing. Period.

When we ignore the fullness of God's truth and instead water down His message to make it more user-friendly, we'll find ourselves in trouble. Half-truths are half-lies. And since our identities are found in Him, how can we live authentically when our understanding of God is laced with untruths? We can't.

I can think back to plenty of times when I doubted God and His promises for my life. I've been angry with Him because He didn't answer my prayers how I wanted them answered. I have purposefully turned away from Him, having a good ole temper tantrum. And in those moments I was only half believing He loved me. I was only half believing He was for me. I was essentially calling God a liar.

I may not have said it to His face, but my unbelief said it for me. I bet you've been there too. Gosh, haven't we all?

You see, being unafraid to live authentically means we believe God all the time and in every situation. It means we believe we are who He says we are, and we believe God is who He says He is. Believing changes everything.

In Mark 5 we meet the woman with this issue of bleeding. If you remember, for twelve years she bled nonstop. It made her unclean and therefore an outcast in society. And when doctors and treatments failed, she put all her hope in Jesus.

As He was passing by, she reached out and touched the hem of His robe. At once He stopped and asked, "Who just touched My robe?" (v. 30 VOICE). Here's what happened next in verses 32–34:

> **Woman:** *I touched You.*
> *Then she told Him the reason why. Jesus listened to her story.*
> **Jesus:** *Daughter, you are well because you* dared to believe. *Go in peace, and stay well.*

She dared to believe. What a beautiful phrase that proved enough to heal her body, soul, and mind. What if we dared to believe we are who God says we are? What if we believed we were made on purpose and for a purpose? What if we decided to trust Him rather than be afraid to be our real selves? What if we stopped believing untruths that say we're too much or not enough?

Let's choose to believe God's truth so we can live authentic.

When We Believe Lies Others Say about Us

Many of us grew up with hurtful words being thrown at us. Even if they were couched in "constructive criticism" or passed off as "just a joke," deep down they still hurt. Maybe the intent wasn't for them to hurt our feelings, but they did.

People we trusted said insensitive things that knocked us to our knees. Others labeled us with lies about who we are. And because we didn't know better, we believed them. We may have started out thinking we were okay, but it never takes long for the world to beat us up. Somewhere along the way we forgot we're deeply loved and valued by our Creator.

Jump ahead to middle school and high school, and those lies were amplified. Can you think of any other time in life when we've struggled more to fit in? We ran into mean girls and out-for-one-thing boys, and the untruths sank deeper into our DNA.

By the time we limped into adulthood, we'd lost sight of who we were. We forgot that God created us on purpose. We decided our failures and disappointments defined us. We stopped believing God delighted in us. We remembered the unkind words spoken about us. And we forgot that being unique and special is by design. We allowed the wounding words of others to become labels, and we've been wearing them for years.

Who or what have others said you are? *Unlovable? Unacceptable? Unworthy? Annoying? Too much? Not enough?* If you're believing these kinds of lies, you've made an agreement somewhere along the way. You decided they were right. Rather than fact-check, you adopted their assessment of who you are as truth. And these lies and labels have a powerful way of keeping the real you tucked away.

Think about it. What agreements have you made? Ask God to give you the grit and grace to unearth these untruths. If we continue allowing the opinions of others to define who we are, we're in big trouble. God has the monopoly on that information. And He wants us to believe we are who He says we are so we'll have the confidence to live authentic lives pleasing to Him.

What's at the Root of All the Lies?

Now that we've established how lies make their way into our lives, let's dig a little deeper. What is the source of all lies? We touched on this a little at the beginning, but I want us to unpack it in greater detail right now.

We have a real enemy who hates us. It's Satan. God is who he despises the most, but since he can't hurt the Almighty, he goes after the next best thing—His children.

For most of my life, I have agreed with who the Enemy said I was. Regardless of whose lips spoke those mean-spirited words to me, I know who authored them. I know where they originated. I didn't always, but I do now.

I'm not letting my accusers off the hook. They chose to partner with evil and said those hurtful things. But have you ever heard the saying, "Don't kill the messenger"? Friend, we must recognize who the real enemy is. It's key to unbelieving untruths. Unless we know a liar is walking the perimeter of our lives, looking for a way to get in and discourage us, we'll miss this silent killer.

Knowledge is power.

I've always known my son has a special calling on his life. I can't explain why I believe this, but I do. I've even had godly friends see that same truth and share it with me unprompted. Complete strangers have even told me (and him) they see it too. That means Satan knows it as well, and he's been bringing chaos into Sam's life since the day he was born.

Because of some health issues, we were told having children would be almost impossible on our own and would more than likely require medical intervention. But God had different plans, and we got pregnant soon after we were married.

I remember sitting in the hospital bed after the C-section birth, watching Sam sleeping, tucked away in his bassinet.

Wayne was sitting in the chair next to me, and we were both in awe. The nurse came in to check vitals, and as he was standing over Sam, commenting on how great he was doing, Sam's arms went into the air, and they began to shake.

In our naivety, my husband and I commented on how adorable it was. We were so enamored with every motion or noise that child made. But the nurse screamed out, "He's not breathing!" Immediately, he flipped Sam over and began to pound on his back as he ran out the door with him. I sat there stunned, and my husband ran out the door behind them.

I cannot find the right words to express how I felt in that moment. It's so painful and scary to reconnect with those feelings—those fears—even now. And I know some of you are nodding your heads and fighting back tears because you know firsthand the complexity of what I'm sharing.

Sam struggled to breathe on his own for days. Because I didn't have contractions during birth, the fluid in his lungs wasn't able to work its way out naturally and was causing issues now. He was struggling to catch his breath and had to be on oxygen. That delayed our homecoming, which was followed by more doctor visits in the days to come.

It broke me. I was healing from surgery, feeling helpless, and listening to the lie that said I was undeserving of good things. The lies told me I was the reason Sam was struggling to breathe—that I had done something wrong—so I felt guilty. I agreed with the lie that said I wasn't good enough to be a mom. And in my fear, I made an agreement with evil.

John 8:45 (MSG) says this of the Enemy: "He couldn't stand the truth because there wasn't a shred of truth in him. When the Liar speaks, he makes it up out of his lying nature and fills the world with lies." This verse offers us some powerful understanding of what we're dealing with.

It tells us the following:

- Satan can't stand truth.
- There is no truth in him.
- He makes up lies.
- He has a lying nature.
- He fills the world with lies.

I believe that while others may speak discouragement and despair into our lives, and while we may beat ourselves up at the drop of a dime, the Enemy is the source of it all. His plan all along has been to make us doubt ourselves so we'll live in counterfeit ways. And he wants to stop us from living authentic because he knows the power we'll have if we embrace our true identities.

So What Do We Do?

We talked earlier about having the mind of Christ and how it's available to us through the Holy Spirit. Well God is very clear in His Word about protecting our thought life. And one of my favorite verses that addresses this is Proverbs 4:23 (GNT): "Be careful how you think; your life is shaped by your thoughts." The author is telling us that more than anything we care for, more than anything we defend, our minds should be at the top of the list. How we think becomes how we act. If we believe who we really are is good, our words and actions will reflect it. But if we believe the lies that say we're worthless, our response to the world will reflect it.

You know, *guard* isn't a passive word. It's an active verb, and it takes grit and grace to walk this out. We're called to watch over our minds with resolve. The opposite of *guard* is *neglect*, and that's what gets us into trouble. We must choose between our options every day: we will either guard or neglect the truth.

While I appreciate the directness of Proverbs 4:23, I struggle to walk this out. Sometimes neglecting is easier than guarding. Amen? And it's usually because of neglect that I start praying for the mind of Christ like we discussed earlier in this chapter. Sometimes our best-laid plans to stand guard fail, and the lies sneak right past our best defenses and into our hearts.

The results can be devastating and might look just like this eight-step train wreck:

> Step 1: We let down our guard and start ruminating over the hurtful words from others.
> Step 2: Those lies become our truth because we decide to believe them.
> Step 3: Our self-worth takes a huge hit and we get tangled in our insecurities.
> Step 4: We begin to beat ourselves up, feeling inadequate and unacceptable.
> Step 5: Fear creeps in, making us feel vulnerable.
> Step 6: Then up go our walls of self-protection.
> Step 7: We start acting differently, more guarded with our words and calculated with our actions.
> Step 8: We shut down, push community away, and hide.

At the end is the incentive we need to live counterfeit lives rather than authentic ones. All this mess is because we let a negative thought or two get away from us. Yuck. I don't want to live this way anymore. Do you?

Let's choose to guard our hearts from lies, because they're huge barriers to authentic living. Let's ask God to unearth the untruths we're believing so we can be confident. And let's remember who the real enemy is so we can forgive people for speaking hurtful things into our lives.

THE TRUTH CHANGES THINGS

Psalm 86:11 says, "Teach me your way, O LORD, so that I may live in your truth. Focus my heart on fearing you" (GW). This should be the cry of our hearts and part of our battle plans. Here's why I love this verse so much:

- The author recognizes the need for God's guidance to navigate life.
- He knows God's truth is key to living authentic.
- He understands that fearing (respecting) God keeps us from fearing (being afraid of) man.

Based on this verse, I'm going to drop a heavy truth on you, knowing this piece of information matters if we're really serious about living authentic. Here it is: You cannot *live* an authentic life unless you are willing to *see* life authentically.

In other words, if you choose to see yourself, your circumstances, and your relationships filtered through the lens of untruths, you won't see them accurately. And how can we be authentic women when truth isn't our guide? When we don't see things the way they really are, we tend to make bad decisions. And those bad decisions come with consequences many of us don't want to pay.

How many times have we lashed out in anger or cut off community only to discover our reason was bogus? Think of the times we've gossiped about someone who hurt us and then realized their offense was unintentional. When we react to untruths in hurtful ways, we aren't being authentic, because God didn't make us to exact revenge. He made us to love others, finding the grit and grace to be kind and compassionate even when the situation doesn't call for it. He wants us to be truth seekers.

In John 8:31–32, Jesus reminds us of something amazing. He's talking to a group of Jewish men struggling to make the connection between Jesus and God. That chapter is worth the read to get a better understanding of context. But the part I want to highlight here is when He said to them, "If you hear My voice and abide in My word, you are truly My disciples; you will know the truth, and that truth will give you freedom" (voice).

I just love this. What a beautiful reminder that when we believe God—believe He is who He says He is and that we are who He says we are—it will free us up to live the way He intended. If we'll let it, His truth will trump the lies we've adopted.

There's an all-out assault on your heart and mind because the Enemy is afraid you will find out who you really are. He's scared you'll find the confidence to walk out God's plans for your life. And he's been trying to take you down any way he can with discouragement, disappointment, defeat, disillusionment, and doubt.

He uses these tactics to keep you from being the courageous woman God intended. The Enemy wants to shut you down so you'll never embrace the path He intended you to walk. He attacks because he's scared of your potential. And he does this through lies whispered into your heart at just the right time.

Friend, you don't have to agree with those lies anymore. And if you are going to live an authentic life, be unafraid to deal with them here and now. It will take grit and grace, but you have both.

Let Galatians 5:1 be an ever-present reminder: "Freedom is what we have—Christ has set us free! Stand, then, as free people, and do not allow yourselves to become slaves again" (GNT). You get to choose whether you thrive or just survive. You get to choose whether you guard your heart or neglect it. You get to choose whether you adopt the mind of Christ or entertain the Enemy's lies. Choose freedom!

Only God's truth will free you from the lies. And the one thing that will keep you in captivity is continuing to agree with those lies. It's time to unearth the untruths so you can live an authentic life that reflects who God made you to be.

You are not the sum of your mistakes. You are not a collection of your failures. And when you allow God to open your eyes to the truth, you can face life unafraid.

FINDING THE GRIT

Can you think of a time you entertained the Enemy's lies? What did that look like?

What are the biggest lies the Enemy whispers to you? How have you handled his lies in the past?

What were your thoughts on asking God for the mind of Christ? How would that change things for you?

Are you going to take the twenty-four-hour challenge to keep track of the hurtful things you say to yourself? What might this uncover for you?

We talked a lot about Satan in this chapter. What did you learn? What empowered you?

How does unearthing the untruths help you live an authentic life?

FINDING THE GRACE

Father, I realize how many lies I listen to in my life. I confess that I've allowed them to be bigger than Your truth, and I am sorry. My desire is to be a truth seeker, and I'm asking You to help me discern the difference. Help me guard my heart so I don't fall prey to the Enemy's schemes to discourage me. I want to live a life that's exactly what You planned for me. I don't want to settle for counterfeit living, because it's in the opposite direction of Your plan. Give me the courage to unearth the untruths, and please replace those lies with Your truth. I want to have the mind of Christ! In Jesus' mighty name, amen.

Live

Accept Your Awesomeness

Unearth the Untruths

T

H

E

N

T

I

C

CHAPTER 6

Try Loving Everyone

*Live in such a way that if someone spoke
badly of you, no one would believe it.*
—Author Unknown

I sat next to my friend, listening to the words coming from her mouth, and my jaw dropped. I was speechless. I literally couldn't find any words to speak.

You know those times when a piece of truth drops into your lap, completely catching you off guard? When new information is so powerful that it shifts your whole understanding of a situation? When this revelation makes you take a detour from where you thought things were? Yeah, this was one of those moments.

As we sat there, my heart began to sink as red-hot anger began to rise. I was shocked. To learn how a mutual "friend" had been trash-talking me for months rocked my world— in a bad way. She had been sloppy sweet to my face but mean-spirited behind my back. Even more, she was speaking bad about my daughter too.

Now maybe your reaction would be different in a situation like this, but that information didn't sit well with me. I mean, say what you want about me, but bringing my daughter into it is a whole new ball game. Amen? Especially when what was being said wasn't fair or true about either of us. Situations like this fast-track me into mama-bear mode, and it ain't pretty. No way. No how.

I thought back to a conversation with this woman several months earlier when I'd found the grit and grace to extend an olive branch—*again*. She and I had a history of disagreements. And while I know I can be wretched and nasty and snarky, she makes me look like an amateur. A neophyte. A freshman. Green as green gets. It's just the truth. And because our circles were going to intersect again, I asked God to help me forgive and move forward. He did, and I did too.

At some point, isn't it His plan for us to mature enough that we can access grace when we need it? Aren't we supposed to become women who let go of the past and move on to greener pastures? Aren't we to outgrow the childishness and embrace adulting so we can thrive in community and love one another?

Yes, I think that's what Jesus meant when He said, "If it is within your power, make peace with all people" in Romans 12:18 (VOICE). This is a beautiful call for us to rise above our differences and come together. But this chapter in Romans is also full of other ways we can love and honor people. It tells us:

- *If people mistreat or malign you, bless them. Always speak blessings, not curses* (v. 14).

- *Work toward unity, and live in harmony with one another. Avoid thinking you are better than others or wiser than the rest; instead, embrace common people and ordinary tasks* (v. 16).
- *Do not retaliate with evil, regardless of the evil brought against you. Try to do what is good and right and honorable as agreed upon by all people* (v. 17).
- *Again, my loved ones, do not seek revenge; instead, allow God's wrath to make sure justice is served. Turn it over to Him. For the Scriptures say, "Revenge is Mine. I will settle all scores"* (v. 19).
- *Never let evil get the best of you; instead, overpower evil with the good* (v. 21).

Well I didn't want to do any of these things. I concocted a plan that looked very different, and in that moment I wanted to trash-talk her right back to anyone who would listen. Hearing the words she had been spewing about me and my girl felt like a slap in the face. I was embarrassed that I'd been oblivious, having no idea that she was being so mean-spirited one minute and bringing me coffee the next.

I've heard some say time heals, implying we'll eventually forget the offense and move on from it. That it won't have power over us anymore and our hearts will soften or open up again. Yes, I think that's the idea. But unless we ask God to heal us from the inside out, things may never change. Tangled people tangle people, and only God can loosen those knots.

I'm sure you have your own story of a situation like this. There's no shortage of mean girls. But let's be honest. Not only do we have a story or two about being treated this way, but we've often been the ones to treat others in less than lovey ways too. None of us are above snarky. We're just not. But it's scary to watch our society thrive on mean-spiritedness in what seems like even bigger doses than before. It seems the more the world tells us to have tolerance, the less tolerant we are becoming. The more people demand respect and equality, the less inclined we are to give it. It's messed up.

When I'm being mean toward or dismissive of someone, I'm not living my authentic self. I'm not being true to who I am, because when I chose to become a Jesus-girl, I was given the divine ability to treat others with respect. And you were too.

> The Holy Spirit produces a different kind of fruit: unconditional love, joy, peace, patience, kindheartedness, goodness, faithfulness, gentleness, and self-control. You won't find any law opposed to fruit like this. (Galatians 5:22–23 VOICE)

These characteristics of Jesus are available to us every day and in every situation. We can choose to use them, or we can choose not to. Sometimes it's easy to pluck this fruit from the vine, and other times we don't even reach for it. Regardless, you and I have full access to it. And it's what helps us treat others with respect, even when they don't deserve it.

But let's dig a little deeper. Fruit is the result of something grown. God doesn't give us the seeds of the Spirit. No. We are given the fruit. But these characteristics take time to grow within us. And even more, it's the Holy Spirit in us that makes these Jesus-like characteristics mature.

Here's what I love about this process. The responsibility

isn't on us to cultivate by our own strength. Through both good and hard times, these fruits are *grown*. We don't plant a seed one day and pick fruit the next. We wait for it. We watch for it. The growing season endures both goodness and adversity. And then we see the fruit with our own eyes, watching as it begins to grow. Even then, we wait for it to mature into what it's supposed to be. It's not a quick process, but it is worth the wait.

Our job is to surrender to the growing process, letting the Spirit prune and weed as necessary. We trust God through the rainy and dry seasons. Remember, it's not about us making the fruit grow—we're not that powerful. It's about us allowing the Gardener to do what He does best.

Let's look at the fruit in detail, and how we can use each one to bless others.

UNCONDITIONAL LOVE

The Greek word that defines this kind of love is *agape*. It's interesting to note that this isn't a feeling but a choice—a big, hairy choice that takes grit and grace to walk out, for sure. We can all love conditionally, but it takes some serious Jesus-infusion for us to love *unconditionally*. Only He can keep our hearts for others steady when we're ready to rock the boat by talking smack.

The trouble is many of us allow our feelings to mandate our love for others. Aren't there times you just don't *feel* like loving someone? I don't always feel like loving my kids. Sometimes I'm so angry with my husband that I don't feel like loving him either. When friends hurt me, I want to reject them right back. Feelings can get us in so much trouble. Amen?

But this agape love is a choice we make to give up our needs and desires to help fulfill someone else's. It's not easy. Not at all. And God must have known this, which is why He asks the Holy Spirit to help us make the hard choice to love. . .anyway.

You're going to love this next part. I discovered that when we run across scripture that requires us to make a choice to love or not, it's the agape kind of love it's talking about. It looks like this:

We agape (choose to love) **God.**
You see, to love God means that we keep His commands, and His commands don't weigh us down. (1 John 5:3 voice)
We agape (choose to love) **our friends.**
There is no greater way to love than to give your life for your friends. (John 15:13 voice)
We agape (choose to love) **our enemies.**
If you want to be extraordinary—love your enemies! Do good without restraint! Lend with abandon! Don't expect anything in return! Then you'll receive the truly great reward—you will be children of the Most High—for God is kind to the ungrateful and those who are wicked. (Luke 6:35 voice)
We agape (choose to love) **everyone else.**
The central truth—the one you have heard since the beginning of your faith—is that we must love one another. (1 John 3:11 voice)

We get to choose if we're going to love others. Some will be easy to love, others will most certainly not. But God has placed in us the fruit of love that will be grown. We may not possess it right now, but we will. And if we're going to be women who live authentic lives, we have to ask the Holy Spirit to make this fruit come alive in our hearts. Then we can muster the grit and grace to love the unlovable and lovable alike.

Choosing to show others unconditional love is one of the most amazing things we can do for them. Even more, we are saying *yes* to authentic living because we are being true to our real selves.

JOY

Just like unconditional love, joy is a choice. That means we can decide we don't want it or won't allow it to manifest in our lives. Instead, we can choose to be victims, see the glass half-empty, mope around, and let that nastiness be directed toward everyone we know. But that is not who you and I were created to be. It's not our true self. It's not authentic.

The Greek word for joy is *chara*. This kind of joy is the result of us letting God be at work in our lives. And every time we see *chara* in scripture, it's because God initiated it. I'm glad it's not our responsibility to create it, because sometimes the last thing we feel is joy. Right? You see, His actions are the basis for our joy, what make it possible. From the birth of Jesus (Luke 1:14) to His resurrection (Matthew 28:8) to our own salvation (Acts 13:52), God's actions are what supply our joy. How can they not?

But what makes joy so challenging for us is that society tells us joy is found in material things. So we spend our time and treasure on items that promise to fill that empty space inside. What we need is more Jesus, but we're told the new car, the cute haircut, the trendy bag, the cool jacket, or the tricked-out phone will give us the emotional boost we crave. But in the end, those fixes are short-term and we find ourselves back to square one—discouraged and unfulfilled. We're left joyless.

If there's anything the world needs right now, it's a big dose of joy. And since we were created to be joy carriers, we need to ask the Lord to give it to us. He is the only one who can fill us up long-term. And when we have Spirit-grown joy inside, we become a blessing to those around us—just like we were created to be.

Peace

One of the fruits I pray for the most is peace. With the world as crazy as it is and with chaos at almost every turn, I crave this in my heart more than anything else. And when I have peace inside me, I can pass that peace on to others.

Think about it. When you're in a frantic state and someone reminds you that God is already in the middle of your situation, something in your spirit shifts. I believe that's because of the promise from Isaiah 26:3 that reads, "You will keep the peace, a perfect peace, for all who trust in You, for those who dedicate their hearts and minds to You" (voice). Regardless of what is happening in the natural, we have access to supernatural peace anytime, anywhere.

And when we grab onto that promise from Isaiah, we can then be agents of peace for others, a beautiful gift we can offer those around us. And as we're learning, we have the power to choose peace-filled lives because the Holy Spirit faithfully matures the fruit God has already given us. Embracing it is another step toward authentic living because we're accepting who we were created to be—and using it to bless others.

PATIENCE

You're going to love this. The Greek word for the kind of patience listed in Galatians 5:22 is *makrothumia*. This word is a combination of *makros*, which means long, and *thumos*, which means passion or temper. So the patience listed in the fruit of the Spirit literally means *a long temper*. In other words, someone who has *makrothumia* isn't quick to unleash on someone. They are slow to anger. Friend, this fruit is a little slow growing in me.

Because this is a fruit—and just like we've learned about the fruit already discussed—it's available to us only through the power of God's Holy Spirit. Amen to that. While I may pray the most for peace, maybe patience should top my list.

May I just be real with you for a minute? I know we are called to be patient, and I know that because of God we *can* be patient, but I struggle with this so much. Here's my ugly admission. I scream at drivers—not really so they know I'm screaming at them, but those in my car do. I lose my patience so fast, especially when they don't go the speed limit or wait too long to push the gas after the light has turned green. Seriously. I'm not alone, right?

But no matter how I justify it (and I've tried!), this is not treating others with respect even though choosing patience in a world full of annoyance is hard. Yet we have the power to choose patience anyway. Why? Because patience is a gift from God and grown in us through the Holy Spirit. However, we must choose it. And for many of us, it takes all the grit and grace we can find to muster *makrothumia*.

Patience comes from a position of power and authority because it's full of self-control. We may choose patience because we know our children will eventually remember to clean up their rooms without reminders. We may choose patience because we know our husbands didn't mean to forget that item from the grocery store. And choosing patience and compassion is a beautiful way to show others there is grace and forgiveness, and even room for second chances. Having patience reminds them that perfection isn't an expectation and mess-ups are acceptable.

And this fruit is part of who we are, because God gave it to us at creation.

KINDHEARTEDNESS

In the King James Version of the Bible, kindness is referred to as gentleness. And in the original Greek, the word for kindness is *chrēstotēs*, which means "excellence, goodness, benignity, and uprightness."[9] It's also defined as empathy, concern, and warmheartedness. Talk about a gift to share with others.

Kindness is a powerful tool and a weapon to battle discouragement. Think about it. Few things can make us feel more loved and seen than an act of kindness, be it random or targeted toward us. And we can make someone's day by picking this fruit and passing it along. But sometimes we misuse it, having the wrong motives behind our kindness.

We might be kind to get our way or fake our sympathy all for show—and it can devastate someone's heart in the process. What we need to understand is how we can be kind like God. The kindness He has shown His children is unimaginable.

When sin separated us from God, in His kindness He made a way to bridge that gap through Jesus. Romans 5:8 says, "But God showed his great love for us by sending Christ to die for us while we were still sinners" (TLB).

In His kindness, God handmade us for good things. Ephesians 2:10 says, "For we are the product of His hand, heaven's poetry etched on lives, created in the Anointed, Jesus, to accomplish the good works God arranged long ago" (VOICE).

Because He is so kind to us, God meets our every need. Psalm 23:2–3 says, "He provides me rest in rich, green fields beside streams of refreshing water. He soothes my fears; He makes me whole again, steering me off worn, hard paths to roads where truth and righteousness echo His name" (VOICE).

We were created to be kind to others, even to those we think don't deserve it. It's part of our authentic selves. And while being kind can offer challenges, remember the Holy Spirit is growing and maturing this fruit in you. Because of that, we can choose to pluck it when we need it.

And honestly, how might our world be a better place if we chose to extend kindness to those around us?

GOODNESS

One of my favorite passages is Matthew 5:13–16. My book *Uncommon* is anchored in it. It's a perfect picture of why our goodness matters.

> *You, beloved, are the salt of the earth. But if salt becomes bland and loses its saltiness, can anything make it salty again? No. It is useless. It is tossed out, thrown*

away, or trampled. And you, beloved, are the light of the world. A city built on a hilltop cannot be hidden. Similarly, it would be silly to light a lamp and then hide it under a bowl. When someone lights a lamp, she puts it on a table or a desk or a chair, and the light illumines the entire house. You are like that illuminating light. Let your light shine everywhere you go, that you may illumine creation, so men and women everywhere may see your good actions, may see creation at its fullest, may see your devotion to Me, and may turn and praise your Father in heaven because of it. (VOICE)

Oh, I love this. We could do nothing more loving for those we have the privilege of influencing than pointing them to God. This passage says our words and actions have the power to direct others to the Lord. That's goodness at its very core.

And as you and I know—because we can be a little snarky and full of attitude—the only way our lives can steer anyone toward God is through the help of the Holy Spirit. You see, goodness as a fruit of the Spirit means *beneficial results*—the good things matured in us by God. And believe me, anything good you see in me is there *only* because of God.

So once again we see this fruit isn't something we have to strive for; goodness is something we must allow the Holy Spirit to mature in us. We have access to it, but we must choose to use it. And when we do, our realness shines through.

Faithfulness

Faithfulness means we believe that God is who He says He is, and that He will do what He says He will do.

Faithfulness means we believe the Bible to be 100 percent God-breathed. It means we know that God is reliable, so we trust His timing and His plan. And, friend, trusting like this is so hard to do.

Remember, God gave us the Holy Spirit, and in turn He gives us the ability to have this kind of faith. We simply cannot create faithfulness on our own because too many distractions cultivate fear and insecurity. Every day, we must choose the faithfulness available through the Holy Spirit, because every day we face impossibilities. We must ask the Spirit to activate our ability to trust God.

Have you ever read Hebrews chapter 11? It's one of those crazy-cool passages of scripture, and it's been nicknamed the Hall of Faith. Please make the time to read it, because it will deeply encourage you.

We learn about some well-known Old Testament characters like Noah, Abraham, Sarah, Joseph, Moses, and even the prostitute Rahab. These men and women *by faith* trusted God in their crazy circumstances. And I'm glad He included this part of their story in His.

Listen, just because they're in the Bible doesn't mean they're better than you and me. They dealt with the same insecurities and fears and every other kind of self-esteem-tangling struggle in their day as we do in ours. Knowing that everyday people just like you and me could choose to trust God over their circumstances gives me the courage to trust Him too.

And check this out. Verse 6 reads, "Without faith no one can please God because the one coming to God must believe He exists, and He rewards those who come seeking" (VOICE). This verse gives us some pretty powerful truth to chew on:

- We can't please God if we are faithless.
- We must believe He is real so we can reach out to Him.
- We are rewarded for seeking Him.

Even more, being steadfast in our faith is a blessing to those around us. Our ability and willingness to trust God gives others strength to do the same. Friend, you and I were created to have that kind of faith. It's who we really are— our authentic selves. And when we operate in that authenticity made possible by the Spirit, we encourage others to rely on God more than themselves.

GENTLENESS

Some translations call gentleness, meekness. Honestly, I used to think meekness was just another way to say weakness. And so I wanted nothing to do with it. But it's not that at all. I'm learning it takes great courage and strength to show gentleness in a world that can often beat the stuffing out of us.

Titus 3:2 reminds us what gentleness looks like. "Don't tear down another person with your words. Instead, keep the peace, and be considerate. Be truly humble toward everyone" (VOICE). Let's break this down.

The fruit of gentleness helps us:

- Use our words wisely.
- Work toward harmony with others.
- Treat others with respect and thoughtfulness.
- Be others-focused rather than self-focused.

But let's be realistic. Can we all agree that our only hope for this kind of living is with help from the Holy Spirit? He is the one to grow this divine characteristic within us, while we have the burden of choosing to use it.

When we do use it, though, it is such an encouragement to those around us. Can you think of people in your life who express gentleness with you? I sure can, and they are some of my favorite people.

SELF-CONTROL

Many of us may need this one the very most. Do I hear an amen in the house? Self-control is simply the ability to control ourselves. It's choosing not to make that mean-spirited comment when the situation tells you it's warranted. It's deciding not to throw the lamp across the room in frustration. It's taking a deep breath instead of giving someone a piece of your mind. It's choosing the grilled chicken over the meat-lovers pizza. It's buying the cute, trendy purse at Target instead of the out-of-your-budget bag from Coach. Self-control is choosing to say no when we'd rather say yes to our human desires.

It's why we can turn from sin.

And our ability to have self-control is only because the Holy Spirit helps grow this fruit in us. He is why we have the strength not to act out of our fleshy desires. But even then, it's not easy. As with all the other fruit, whether to exercise self-control is a hard choice we must make. Even Paul—an amazing pillar in the faith—struggled with doing the right thing. Listen to him unpack his struggle in Romans 7:21–25.

Here's an important principle I've discovered: regardless of my desire to do the right thing, it is clear that evil is never far away. *For deep down I am in happy agreement with God's law; but the rest of me does not concur. I see a very different principle at work in my bodily members, and it is at war with my mind; I have become a prisoner in this war to the rule of sin in my body. I am absolutely miserable! Is there anyone who can free me from this body where sin and death reign so supremely? I am thankful to God for the freedom that comes through our Lord Jesus, the Anointed One!* So on the one hand, I devotedly serve God's law with my mind; but on the other hand, with my flesh, I serve the principle of sin. (VOICE, emphasis mine)

We may want to do what is good and right, but the pull of sin is strong. And everywhere. Maybe this is exactly why God decided His Spirit needed to be the one to develop self-control in us, rather than simply relying on our own willpower. Smart move, eh?

You know why this fruit helps others so much? It's because of the power of a testimony. Something happens when we know we're not *the only one* to struggle. It helps knowing we're not alone. And supporting one another as we try to be more like Jesus—knowing we're all in the same boat— creates connection and community.

My sister recently lost her father-in-law. I never really got to know Larry, but I always heard wonderful things about him. He loved his wife. He loved his kids. And he was a fabulous grandfather. While he was having a few aches and pains, he was still active and happy. So when the doctor diagnosed him with cancer, everyone was shocked. Within just a few weeks, Larry had gone to be with the Lord.

At the last minute, my sister decided to have family and friends over the morning after the memorial service. And when the reality of pulling that off hit her, she freaked out. Of course, she wanted to host the event; that was never a concern. But she was grieving too, and the task felt daunting and overwhelming. She knew she needed help, but like most of us, she struggles to ask for help.

Reluctantly, she sent a text out to her Bible study group, asking if anyone would be willing to drop off some food the following day. And within minutes, her phone was exploding with responses. Stefani was expecting a few women to step up and bring food by, but her entire group rallied around her.

One woman took control and organized the entire event. From the food to the dishes to decorations and everything in between, this group lifted every bit of responsibility off my sister's shoulders. No doubt, they'd experienced the loss of someone they loved. They must have known the tension between hosting and grieving. And they loved on my sister and her family. They may never know how much their kindness spoke right into her heart.

I believe the Holy Spirit activated the fruit in those Jesus-girls that day.

These nine Christlike characteristics help us become women who can love others well. Because we were created in His image, this fruit of the Spirit proves our faith authentic. It helps us become who God created us to be. It cultivates our true persons, created by God to infuse the world with His goodness. And what a gift when we do.

The fruit of the Spirit is the change in our character that comes about because of the Holy Spirit's work in us. And I don't know about you, but I want to find the grit and grace to reach up and pluck the fruit every day.

FINDING THE GRIT

What fruit of the Spirit was the hardest to read about? And why?

What fresh revelation did God give you in our discussion of the fruit of the Spirit?

We're learning how vital the Holy Spirit is to authentic living. In your own words, how does He make authenticity possible, and why do we need Him?

After reading this chapter, what changes are you going to make in your everyday walk with Jesus?

How does trying to love others help me live authentic?

FINDING THE GRACE

Father, thank You for creating us with the fruit of the Spirit seeds inside. I love how intentional You are to give us exactly what we need to live and love well. And thank You that this fruit isn't something we have to strive for. That makes it all the better! I appreciate that this fruit is the Holy Spirit's domain, and He is the one who matures them in us. Father, would You help me love others like You love us? Would you help me always choose to pluck the fruit I need each day? I want to be a woman whose heart for community points others to You in heaven. I love you so much. In Jesus' mighty name I pray, amen.

Live
Accept Your Awesomeness
Unearth the Untruths
Try Loving Everyone
H
E
N
T
I
C

CHAPTER 7

Hold on to Hope

Forget all the reasons why it won't work
and believe the one reason why it will.
—Ziad K. Abdelnour[10]

We've discovered that while I may be the best driver in the family, I'm most certainly *not* the best driving instructor. Oh no, not at all. That award goes to my husband, who doesn't scream curse words when our fifteen-year-old takes the corner too fast. I may or may not have said a choice word or two while holding on to the dashboard for dear life. Sweet mother, I think I need therapy.

Truth is, my son isn't a bad driver. He's actually quite good. And while he may take a corner a little faster than feels comfortable to me, we're not in jeopardy of rolling over. He may still be in learning mode, but the kid is doing a bang-up job (in a good way) of learning how to navigate the road and a vehicle. Of course, all credit goes to my husband, who never seems to get his feathers ruffled during those drives.

For me, these drives are full of all kinds of hopes.

I hope Sam will stay on the road.

I hope he'll remember his turn signal and to check the other lane before he moves into it.

I hope I can speak lovingly to him during this nail-biting drive.

I hope I don't die.

And I'm sure Sam has one prevailing hope: *I hope my mom will keep her mouth shut.*

Hope is a powerful motivator. It's what drives us to try again. It's what keeps us from sinking under the weight of adversity. Hope keeps us positive, fuels our joy, and helps us reach for our dreams with gusto. Hope matters. And while many think hope is nothing more than wishful thinking, the biblical definition is quite different. Christian hope means *confident expectation.* It's believing in the possibility.

But honestly, it takes hard-won grit and grace to hold on to hope in this world. Grit, because sometimes we'd rather give up than white-knuckle it. Aren't there moments it would just be easier to throw in the towel? And we need grace for ourselves, because sometimes we don't walk it out as well as we'd like. Holding on to hope is just plain hard— no matter how you slice it.

But listen in real close. If we're going to live authentic lives—lives true to who we were made to be—then we need to remember that hope is already part of our DNA. Because we're created in God's image, hope is already part of our blueprint. So while it may be challenging to grab onto hope and hold on, especially when life feels overwhelming, we can absolutely do it. *We must do it.* Friend, holding on to hope is part of what makes you, well, you. And it's a beautiful benefit of being a Jesus-girl.

Have you recognized how strong the connection is between hope and faith? Think about it. You can't have one without the other. Hope is the foundation of your faith just as much as faith is the foundation of your hope. Hope is believing something can or will, and it speaks possibility into our weary hearts.

When I'm sitting in the passenger seat as Sam drives, faith and hope come alive in me. They're why I'll hand the keys over to my fifteen-year-old to begin with. They allow me to believe we'll survive the drive and return home uninjured so I'll be able to have my coffee. Hope helps me have faith in his abilities, and faith ignites my hope. But I can't muster hope and faith on my own. While God Himself is the source of them, it's the Holy Spirit who stirs them in me. Listen to this from Romans 15:13:

> *I pray that* God, the source of all hope, *will infuse your lives with an abundance of joy and peace in the midst of your faith so that your hope will overflow* through the power of the Holy Spirit. (VOICE, emphasis mine)

Here are four meaty truths this verse tells us about hope:

1. God is the source of it.
2. It partners with faith.
3. We can have it in abundance.
4. The Holy Spirit awakens it.

This scripture also confirms in me a powerful combination

that starts with God and ends with God. This recipe has all the right ingredients, and it's worthy of chewing on. Check this out:

God created us to hope.
And it's faith that makes hope possible.
The result is a willingness to trust God,
Because we know God is our only hope.

It's a full-circle process that begins and ends with God. Yes, and amen. He is hope, and the relationship between that and faith is magnificent and potent. But hope is so much more. Have you ever thought about all the ways it intersects with your life? The Word of God is chock-full of the details, but here are a few of my favorites:

God's plan for your life includes hope (Jeremiah 29:11).

He created hope to fulfill your deepest needs (Romans 5:5).

Hoping (trusting) in God will renew your strength (Isaiah 40:31).

Hope reminds you of possibility (Mark 9:23).

Hoping in God alone brings blessings (Jeremiah 17:7).

The Word of God is meant to give you hope (Romans 15:4).

Hope makes you confident and courageous (2 Corinthians 3:12).

Your hope in God delights Him (Psalm 147:11).

God created hope to intertwine with every part of our lives, which is why holding on to it makes all the difference in our situations and circumstances. Without hope, we all flounder. Letting go of hope is why we walk out of a hard marriage. It's why we give up on a wayward child. Hopelessness is what makes us reject challenging friendships and step out of frustrating community groups. Losing hope is why we turn our backs on difficult family members, quit frustrating positions of leadership, and let go of a dream that feels too far off. And it is hopelessness that makes people choose to take their own lives.

Haven't we all given up on something or someone, certain a resolution or a common ground was hopeless? We've all faced times when the mountain in front of us seemed too tall to climb again and waving the white flag looked to be the best option. Every one of us has entertained thoughts of giving up and giving in because we've craved the path of least resistance. We want out of the pain. But God didn't create us to be quitters. Your authentic self was designed with a huge dose of hope—hope that encourages you to do what God is asking or requiring.

When I first started writing, I guess I thought it would be easy. I imagined it was just like everything else one does each day—washing dishes, doing laundry, driving carpool. But no, that has never been my experience. Writing always costs me something.

Putting words on a page has never been methodical or mindless or menial for me. When I sit down to write, I *bleed*. I have to dig deep for the grit to open myself up again. And because I mostly write about the hard parts of my story— many of which are the hard parts of most women's stories—I am required to revisit some of my greatest wounding. I have to face heartache all over again.

Writing asks me to reconnect with the deepest parts of my pain. It asks me to emotionally return to places that were incredibly hard. I sit in painful memories, feelings of rejection and betrayal, and I pick at collections of hurts still so raw to the touch. These memories bleed out as my fingers tap the keys on the keyboard. It can be so overwhelming.

I've often wondered why God doesn't ask me to write Amish fiction or share recipes in a cookbook. Maybe it's because I'm not Amish and I don't cook, but honestly, those would be so much easier on my heart. But He doesn't ask the *easy* of me. He asks me to share the details of our private therapy sessions—sacred moments when God and I hash through rough spots and hard spaces. And while I'm not a fan of the process, I'm grateful for the healing that comes on the other side.

My first book was one of these times. *Untangled* was documentation of my healing journey with God. He asked me to share very personal parts of my story in its pages: abuses, failures, fears, shame—all of them. He asked me to be transparent hundreds of miles out of my comfort zone. My hockey-fan husband calls that *leaving everything on the ice*. And in those moments, I wanted to quit because it just felt too vulnerable. I didn't want to revisit those old wounds. But I found the grit to keep the pages open anyway. . .and write.

Untangled didn't get picked up by a publisher for over a year. I received no after no after no, and I had to find the grace to continue believing in that project so I could stay focused and patient. With each heartbreaking rejection, I began to feel hopeless. How could I not? It didn't feel like my book was being rejected; it felt like my story was being rejected. It felt like *I* was being rejected.

So I started asking the hard questions. *Did I really hear God? Does He want me to find a publisher for this book? Is my story worth sharing?*

You know, when someone finds the grit to open up about their messy life, they want others to notice their bravery. Trust me, it's scary to put it all out there. We take a huge risk by sharing personal struggles, and we want to be validated. We want someone to recognize what we just did. We're hoping that we're still loved, that we haven't brought condemnation on ourselves, and that there was a good reason for showing our mess. Hope is why we're able to reveal the hard things.

Hebrews 10:36 says, "Simply endure, for when you have done as God requires of you, you will receive the promise" (VOICE). *Simply endure.* Two little words, one big command. Perseverance takes grit. And it means we choose to tolerate, suffer, withstand, succumb, and put up with. It really is a choice. While we may begin to lose heart, this verse reminds us that staying hopeful in all situations results in a blessing on the other side. And sometimes that's a venti-sized order.

One of the things I appreciate about walking with Jesus is that we have direct access to Him. When we need wisdom, we can get it. When we need comfort, it's available. And when we need hope, it floods into our hearts and cancels the despair we're feeling. All we need to do is ask in faith. That means no matter what comes our way, you and I can find hope in the hard places. Friend, tapping into your God-given access is who you were created to be. Holding on to hope is part of your DNA.

Well, *Untangled* eventually found its way into a publishing house, and God has met countless women in its pages. The book has given me the privilege of connecting with some amazing Jesus-girls—*many with stories like mine.* My heart has been encouraged by their email messages and the stories they've shared with me at events. Even now, years later, the blessings from *simply enduring* are still coming my way. I held on to hope when it would have been easier to fall into a pit. And it's grown my confidence to keep being real in a world of fake.

GIDEON

Gideon needed confidence too. I just love this Bible character. We talked about him in chapter 3, but I want to bring him back into this discussion on hope. He found himself in a tough spot, and hope in God was all Gideon had. Let's dig into his story.

If you remember, in Judges 6, a messenger of God had spoken to Gideon, telling him he was to deliver his people from the Midianites' oppression. We already talked about how while the angel called him *mighty*, he called himself *weak* and *least*. Ring a bell? These statements reveal exactly how Gideon felt about himself. Even more, it tells us how he felt about the situation at hand.

Just to make sure he heard God correctly, he asked for confirmation through dew drops and a wool fleece. We don't have space to unpack that story here, but please check it out in Judges 6:36–40. The bottom line is that Gideon was looking for reassurance. He couldn't hope without it. And God's answer was yes.

With full confidence, Gideon knew God was calling him to deliver Israel from the hands of the Midianites. His hope was anchored in his faith. And the next morning, Gideon stood ready with his mighty army. But then God made changes.

In Judges 7:2–3, God addressed His warrior. "You have too many warriors for Me to allow you to defeat the Midianites. As it is now, the people of Israel would just deny Me the credit and claim they had won the victory on their own. So go out and tell your army, 'Any of you who are afraid and trembling are free to leave Mount Gilead'" (VOICE).

So Gideon did, and twenty thousand men walked away from the camp, leaving ten thousand men for the battle. But then God spoke to Gideon again. "You still have too many warriors. Take them down to the water, and I will sift them for you. When I say, 'This one will fight for you,' he will go with you; but when I say, 'This one will not fight for you,' then he will not go" (v. 4 VOICE).

This is where the story makes me giggle. Did you realize God separated the men based on how they drank the water? They either drank like a dog (on hands and knees, tongue lapping up the water) or they raised their hands up to their mouths. And when they had all satisfied their thirst, the three hundred who drank from their hands were the ones God selected. The rest were sent home. Seriously. I can't make up this stuff.

Now, I'll be honest. I would be super hopeful for a victory knowing I had an army of thirty thousand, not to mention the amazing confirmation from God through the wool fleece petition. I may even remain hope-filled as twenty thousand walked away, knowing I had another ten thousand capable men with me. But my hope probably would have slipped a bit as God whittled my army down to only three hundred.

If I could do math, I'd blow your mind by sharing the big percentage of loss Gideon just suffered. But I'm math-challenged and my husband isn't around. Let's just say *a lot* of Gideon's army was gone—thirty thousand down to three hundred. Yikes. This is where I'd have to dig deep for the grit to stay hopeful and not give in to fear. Maybe you too?

In verses 9–11, God gives the order. "Get up and attack the camp of the Midianites because I have given you victory over them. *But if you should have any fear*, take your servant Purah; scout out the camp, and listen to what they are saying, and afterward you will find you are strong enough to attack" (voice, emphasis mine). Any guesses as to what Gideon did? Yep, he and Purah headed over to the camp for a listen.

This mighty warrior was already struggling with fear, and then he saw how big the Midianite army was. Scripture says there were people as "thick as locusts" and "their camels were as numberless as the sands of the seashore" (Judges 7:12 voice). Gideon had three hundred men, some jars, and some trumpets. *Gulp*. Can you imagine how he must have struggled to hold on to hope? Wouldn't you have?

But God knew his warrior's tendencies. Gideon had just been set up for a divinely orchestrated infusion of hope. He and Purah overheard one of the men sharing with his neighbor his dream that confirmed the Israelites' victory. And this confirmation helped restore Gideon's hope.

Sometimes we just need another shot of faith to keep us encouraged. The two went back, roused their army, and went on to win. But Gideon didn't stop there. Read Judges chapter 8 to get the whole picture. As I mentioned earlier, hope is a powerful motivator.

Gideon was created to be a mighty warrior, but God had to remind him of that reality. It was his true identity, who he was created to be. It was how God saw him regardless of how he saw himself. And choosing to live authentically—choosing to embrace his calling—helped produce the hope he needed to do what God asked. I love every bit of his story.

I wonder, where are you on the hope meter today? Where is God asking you to dig in your heels rather than give in to discouragement? What battle has you holding on for dear life, afraid things won't work out? Where is clinging to hope a desperate battle right now? I know, life is so hard. It's so big sometimes. But never forget God is always *for* you.

Let me interject a permission slip of sorts right here. We've been talking about how authentic living means we hold on to hope no matter what. Why? Because doing so is staying true to how God created us. But, friend, there's no shame in feeling the weight of the battle. There's nothing wrong with feeling discouragement as we try to get back on our feet. Having breakdown moments are part of life, part of humanity. Don't think you're failing to have hope because you had a fleshy moment of despair. Let me share an example.

My kids started a new school year yesterday, and now they're in high school at the same time. How did *that* happen? Sam started his sophomore year in the same school he attended for ninth grade. But as *she* starts ninth grade this year, Sara is in an entirely new school for her—new culture, new people, new hallways, new everything. And when my phone started blowing up with text messages from her asking to come home early on day one, my heart seemed to fall right into my stomach.

I had high hopes this year would be the best for her yet. As I previously shared, several girls at her former school weren't the kindest (why are we women so cruel?). We'd been praying this experience would be different. Be better. Oh, the hours I'd spent begging God for His graciousness toward my daughter. The number of times I'd petitioned Him for a wonderful set of friends, handpicked just for her. There is no doubt we were prayed up and full of sweet expectation!

When her texts came through, I held it together and replied with my best mom advice. I spoke truth and empowered her with each response, trying to infuse hope into her fearful heart. I reminded Sara of who she is because of Jesus, telling her she could do hard things. But my mama heart was in deep anguish. I wanted to pull her from school, wrap her in my arms, and snuggle on the sofa with cookie dough and our favorite movie. And while that would have been awesome, what we both needed the most was to hold on to hope.

I know you have those kinds of moments too. Times when something feels super overwhelming and your first response is to circle the wagons and shut out community. Maybe you are nursing a heart wound or trying to regroup. Regardless, I want to give you permission to be human. Thinking we can always remain positive and hopeful in *this* life is unrealistic. And when we set that expectation and fail (because we will), we end up feeling shame for not being *better*. Don't entertain that lie. It's a setup from the Enemy, designed to take you down.

When I talk about holding on to hope, I'm thinking long-term. It may not be where we start, but this is where we end up.

After Sam and Sara went to bed last night, I sat down in my favorite chair and lost it. My husband sat near me while I purged my tornado of emotions. Yep, it was pretty ugly. I was crying out all my hopelessness. And when I was done, Wayne prayed for me. (I know, he's a good man.) He said, "Honey, tomorrow will be better." In that sweet moment, hope flooded back in. Hope may have slipped for a bit, but I grabbed it and held on.

Because, that's what we do. It's who we are.

Let's unpack three reasons holding on to hope is key to authentic living.

1. Hope helps you see the good.

Being negative is easy because there's a lot to be negative about! Amen? War, politics, sickness, abuse, poverty. Sheesh. It's not hard to fall into the pit of doom and gloom, especially when we give up hope that there is still good in the world.

But you know what? There is *always* good. Sometimes we just have to look for it. I want to challenge you to be a hope hunter and find the goodness the world has to offer. And then be the kind of woman who points out good to others. They need to see it too.

2. Hope reminds you that things can and will get better.

In my book *Uncommon*, I talk about a toy from my childhood called a Weeble. Its tag line was "Weebles wobble, but they don't fall down." Seriously, these toys could not fall over no matter how hard you tried to make them. Their weighted bottoms kept them from lying on their sides. These Weebles are great visuals for hope too.

From time to time, we will get tossed about, face

depressing situations, feel dejected, and see no light at the end of the tunnel. But hope will always remind us that things can and will get better. Why? Because we have God in heaven, who not only hears the cries of His children but also answers them. Isaiah 65:24 confirms it. "I'll anticipate their prayers and respond before they know it; even as they speak, I will hear" (VOICE).

You have a heavenly Father who is always for you. He will restore your hope anytime you need Him to. He'll restore it before you even realize you need it.

3. Hope creates peace in your heart.

Hopelessness is a powerful emotion, creating chaos and conflict in the deepest places of your soul. It magnifies all your feelings of impossibility and despair. And when you have tunnel vision, looking at your situations and circumstances through a narrow lens, hopelessness will make you miserable. Gosh, isn't that the truth! But, friend, hope is powerful too. And it can shift that negativity.

Can you think of a time when something stirred you up, but then a calm came over you as you prayed about it? Or a time when scripture supernaturally leapt off the page and you instantly felt like everything was going to be okay? Or when singing a worship song calmed you down and offered you a new perspective on your situation? Those moments were most certainly infused with God-inspired hope.

There is nothing more amazing than the peace Jesus offers. One of my most prayed prayers is asking for the peace of Jesus to rest on my home, my people, or my heart because I know how mighty that peace can be. Countless studies have shown that hope has positive benefits on our health.

When we hold on to hope, it has both an emotional and a physical effect on our health and our hearts. It's almost like a "buy one, get one free" special!

But sometimes we have to cling to it for dear life.

I'm in the middle of a situation that's threatening to drain every ounce of my hope. Some days it takes all I have to keep a smile on my face and joy in my heart. Some days I feel certain this situation will go my way, but then despair hits and I feel exposed and vulnerable, afraid it may backfire on me. Sometimes I feel sure God is speaking directly to me, giving me signs and messages that everything will work out in my favor. But at other times I'm so confused, wondering if I'm hearing God at all.

So, if you're there right now too, please know you're not alone in the struggle. We're all holding on to hope somewhere. We're all having to find the grit and grace to fight off hopelessness. And each of us must make a daily decision to be real and authentic or to smile and fake it. We are most certainly in this together.

Proverbs 13:12 says, "Hope postponed grieves the heart" (VOICE). Sometimes it's in the waiting that we become hopeless. We don't want to "long-suffer," do we? It's absolutely exhausting when hope is delayed. Waiting is a major hope drainer, and it's not for the faint of heart.

What are you waiting on? Where is your hope postponed right now? Are you holding on to hope for a breakthrough, healing, provision, or forgiveness? For a door to open or close? For results, a promotion, or an answer? For a spouse? To be pregnant? For invitations or opportunities? To have the nerve? For perspective, wisdom, peace, or motivation? Yes, we are all waiting for something—every single one of us. We're all hoping.

But at some point—after grinning and bearing it for so long—the waiting becomes heavy. Hope feels distant. Unreachable. Our resolve to stand steadfast begins to weaken. Grief sets in. Our heart fills with disappointment and discouragement. We struggle to see God in it. Faith begins to wane. And eventually bitterness awakens, anger rises, negativity infiltrates, joy is stolen. . .and hope fades.

We don't get the wool fleece responses like Gideon did.

We don't get to hear the Enemy confirm our victory before the battle like Gideon and Purah did.

We don't get the burning bush experience like Moses did or watch the manna manifest every day like the Israelites in the wilderness did.

We don't get to watch God close the mouths of hungry lions like He did for Daniel.

We don't get to see the hills full of God's army like Elisha's servant did.

We don't get to watch the sea part and then cross on dry ground.

We don't get to watch God manifest as a pillar of fire and of cloud to guide our way like He did during the exodus of His people from Egypt.

Nope. You and I may never have these kinds of divine experiences. But I want you to think of all the times hope did arrive. Remember the times when your situation looked hopeless, but then God changed everything. Remember when you mustered the grit and grace to hold on to hope with all you had and the breakthrough finally came. Remember when God healed and restored? Remember when the door opened or closed? Remember when the answer came? God sees you and me, and he offers us true hope just like He did for those in the Bible.

We may have thought help would never come. We may have complained and thrown a temper tantrum. We may have tried to fix everything ourselves, angry that it seemed God wasn't working in our circumstance. But He always shows up and ignites hope in us when we need it. Read this truth from Psalm 39:7 (TLB). When the psalmist reached the end of his anger and complaining, he made a powerful decision: "And so, Lord, my only hope is in you."

Yes. Friend, your only hope is in the Lord. It has nothing to do with a horoscope. Anchoring your hope in people will set you up for a heartache. It's not dependent on the stock market. No preacher can impart it to you. You cannot work your way toward it in your own strength. You see, I think we've gotten it all wrong, because hoping in *anything* counterfeit or placing our faith in *anyone* other than God will produce short-lived and unfulfilled results.

Life circumstances ebb and flow. They are unpredictable, and life seasons change. But with God we can remain steadfast. When challenges come, it's the perfect time to remind others there's a payoff for sticking it out. This is when we need to encourage others to believe they can do hard things because of Jesus. It's our privilege to model what it looks like to endure so we receive God's blessing on the other side. And when we find the grit and grace to secure our hope in Him, choosing to be honest about our fears and insecurities, we'll have the courage to *simply endure*. We'll have the confidence to live an authentic life full of hope—just like we were created to do.

Let's be warriors of hope to the world.

Don't worry. It's already in you.

FINDING THE GRIT

How do you think hope and faith work together?

What is one change you can make today to help you be more hopeful?

Where do you need to *simply endure,* and what do you think the benefits are if you do?

What did God speak to you through this chapter?

How do you think having hope will help you live authentic?

FINDING THE GRACE

Father, I admit that sometimes holding on to hope feels too hard. While I know You gave me the ability to hope, it's a difficult choice to make when I'm staring at overwhelming situations. Please forgive me for doubting You and struggling to have faith that You'll come through. You are trustworthy and always for me. Help me remember that. Lord, I am asking You to ignite hope within me. When I'm afraid or anxious or discouraged, would You remind me that I have hope already baked into my heart? And when I feel weak and unable to stand, would You strengthen my bones with faith? I need You, Father. I am unable

to navigate this life on my own because hope fades so easily. But I
know that with Your help, I can hold on to hope in the darkest of
times. Thank You for always being with me. I love You so much.
In Jesus' mighty name I pray, amen.

Live
Accept Your Awesomeness
Unearth the Untruths
Try Loving Everyone
Hold on to Hope
E
N
T
I
C

CHAPTER 8

Extend and Embrace Forgiveness

Forgiveness is not an occasional act;
it is a constant attitude.
—Martin Luther King Jr. [11]

*M*y good friend has had to navigate forgiveness with her in-laws. From day one, her husband's mom and sister have treated her unkindly. Even worse, he doesn't stand up to them and defend her. Seventeen years later, she is still dealing with their mean-spiritedness.

Another friend's mom lost her inheritance to a sibling who stole it all. And it was millions of dollars. Even worse, the brother never repented and ended up dying tragically. There was so much pain and zero closure. So many questions were left unanswered. And as a result, forgiveness has not come easily.

Someone else's mother got her involved in a cult and then abandoned her at the age of eleven. The mother basically gave up all parenting rights and left her daughter to fend for herself. As a result, she suffered abuses at the hands of other adults in the group. How do you begin to forgive something like that?

Now, I know this is a crunchy topic. For many of us, it's a complex issue with lots of twists and turns. And our stories are layered with pain and let-downs. Some of you were probably tempted to skip over this chapter. Believe me, I was tempted not to include it in this book. While I've written about unforgiveness extensively in the past, I'm in a tough situation right now where I don't want to forgive. No, not at all.

What was done to me is unforgivable—at least in my opinion. It's betrayal at its core. And honestly, I have every good reason *not* to forgive. But here's where that justification bites me in the behind: I cannot live authentically when I'm harboring unforgiveness in my heart. None of us can. Why? Because it clouds how we see life and how we choose to live each day.

Even more, it adds a filter to our interactions that keep us guarded. We withhold. And we begin to respond in counterfeit ways, careful to measure our words and manage our responses. Friend, it takes real courage to forgive. It can bring up fears, and sometimes it takes every bit of oomph you can muster to extend that kind of unwarranted grace.

Can we be super honest with one another right now? The idea of forgiving is great…until it's your turn. Am I right, or am I right? I easily support the idea of forgiveness till I'm the one who's in the hot seat and needs to extend grace to someone who has hurt me or hurt someone I care about. We can be ready advocates for letting go of offenses until someone disses something we stand for or believe in.

Then the idea of forgiving becomes a whole different beast altogether.

Just the other day, I was trying to find a verse in the Bible to support the idea that forgiveness may be conditional in some situations. I'm not kidding. I wanted to find some divine justification for holding on to anger for an injustice that has overwhelmed me. (Just so you don't get the wrong idea, this has nothing to do with my marriage. I already told you, my man is a rock star.) In God's Word, I wanted to find circumstances where He said forgiveness wasn't warranted or necessary. But then my search brought me back to these verses, and I got stuck.

> **Peter:** *Lord, when someone has sinned against me, how many times ought I forgive him? Once? Twice? As many as seven times?*
> **Jesus:** *You must forgive not seven times, but seventy times seven.* (Matthew 18:21–22 VOICE)

So I did a little math and realized seventy times seven equals 490. And I understood it's not the number that matters. Jesus' point is simple. We're to forgive as many times as it takes. Yuck, but okay.

Then I started down another path. Sometimes I'm persistent in looking for loopholes to support my desire to stick it to the man. Amen? I wondered, since we have to forgive, maybe we can also exert our own punishment to the offender. You know, get in a little dig before we extend grace. That's biblical, right? Sometimes we all need a little taste of our own medicine to learn how others must feel? Surely God would see the value in that plan.

And then here came Paul.

Do not retaliate with evil, regardless of the evil brought against you. Try to do what is good and right and honorable as agreed upon by all people. (Romans 12:17 VOICE)

Ugh. I was back to square one. Then I decided I wouldn't do anything to my offender's face, but I would harbor anger and hate in my own heart toward them. They'd never know I hated them or wanted really bad juju to come their way. They wouldn't feel my wrath; it could just be my little secret. But then this from the book of John got all up in my business.

My commandment to you is this: love others as I *have loved you.* (John 15:12 VOICE, emphasis mine)

Here was my dilemma. How could I secretly hate someone and love them at the same time? I couldn't. Drat, foiled again. I can't act all Christian to my arch nemesis in public and then harbor hate in my heart in private. If I choose this course of action, I'm not being real. I'm being two-faced. And there is nothing authentic about that.

When Jesus says the words *as I* in the verse above, He is telling us to love others like *He* loves us. That leaves no room in our hearts for hate. And even more, we can't love like that in our own strength. We can do it only in His.

Much to my frustration, I was unable to justify unforgiveness. I couldn't rationalize holding on to hate. I couldn't seem to defend my merciless anger. Then I collided with this passage, and I understood why God is so adamant that we forgive.

*When you are angry, don't let it carry you into sin. Don't
let the sun set with anger in your heart or give the devil
room to work.* (Ephesians 4:26–27 VOICE)

Boom. This is compelling to me. This answer to "Why
should I forgive?" paints a powerful picture. And two big
truths stand out:

1. Unforgiveness is a sin.
2. It opens the door for the Enemy.

I've seen this combination at work in my life. Because you're
alive on planet Earth, chances are you have too. When we
make the conscious decision not to forgive, we are sinning.
It goes against what God has commanded us to do. And
holding on to offenses is like placing a key to our hearts into
the hands of the Enemy. We've just granted unlimited access
to someone who hates us and wants to ruin our lives.

Maybe this is why God included Ephesians 4:31–32
in our road map for godly living. These verses don't mince
words. They very clearly tell us what fuels unforgiveness,
what these reactions are laced with, and offer us an alternative way of living—one that creates unity and peace.

*Banish bitterness, rage and anger, shouting and slander,
and any and all malicious thoughts—these are poison.
Instead, be kind and compassionate. Graciously forgive
one another just as God has forgiven you through the
Anointed, our Liberating King.* (VOICE)

This takes courage. This takes grace and grit. It requires authenticity with yourself and others. And with God. It's also

the quickest way to shut down the Enemy and stand firm in your faith.

But what about your heart? I know I've thrown a lot of scripture at you—good, godly wisdom from the Word—but we'd be missing the point if we didn't understand forgiveness from a heart perspective. That's where authenticity lives.

Unforgiveness is very much a heart issue. That's why refusing to extend grace is a dangerous choice. It creates a burden we carry into every nook and cranny of our lives. And unless we find good reason to forgive, our hearts will continue to hold on to the offense and we'll feel justified to act in ways that don't glorify God. That's not how He created us to live. It's not living authentically.

I know you may want to hold on to your anger because resentment feels warranted. I know your annoyance and distress feel defensible. Forgiving stirs up fear that we might get hurt again. But choosing to live an authentic life means that you embrace forgiveness even when it's the last thing you want to do.

Here are nine forgiveness facts:

1. Healing is a by-product of forgiveness.

Did you realize benefits come from forgiving? You see, the quicker we can forgive, the quicker we can heal. Pure and simple. And the quicker we can heal, the truer to our real selves we can stay. Remember, forgiving is always the first step to healing a heart that's been black-and-blued.

2. You benefit the most when you forgive.

As hard as this is to believe, forgiving others has everything to do with you and very little to do with them. When you extend grace, you're literally taking the power away from them to continue hurting you. And because your offender's words or actions can't keep you tangled up any longer, you're now freed up to be who God created you to be.

3. Boundaries can be healthy after forgiveness.

Forgiving doesn't mean you're a doormat. God didn't make you so others could stomp on you all the time. That's not your true self. And sometimes the only way we can release an offense is to put boundaries in place so offenders don't have that kind of access to our hearts. This can often mean that reconciliation with toxic people isn't an option because it isn't safe. And that's called wisdom.

4. Even when you forgive, forgetting isn't always possible.

Remembering a hurt doesn't necessarily mean you're holding a grudge. It just means you are human and have the God-given ability to remember. And sometimes it's those memories that warn you of danger or protect you from further heartache. This helps you navigate tricky situations in genuine ways.

But a red flag—at least for me—is if my anger or bitterness resurfaces when that hurtful situation comes to mind. If I'm still mad about it, chances are I'm still struggling with it.

5. Forgiving doesn't necessarily mean you won't still hurt.

We aren't robots, devoid of emotions. We can't always just let it go. The pain was real and the hurt was deep, so pushing it down and acting like everything is okay isn't authentic or healthy. And we can't just pretend it isn't there when it most certainly is. It's actually beneficial when we can be honest about how we're feeling—honest with ourselves, others, and God. Validated feelings are a step toward forgiveness and healing.

6. Forgiving often requires God's help.

Sometimes forgiveness can happen only with divine intervention. Sometimes the offense is so big and painful that just moving past it is simply beyond our human capabilities. When forgiving feels undoable, God is there to help us. He knows the importance of a healed-up heart, and He is ready to help when we ask. And when we do, He will give us exactly what we need to walk it out.

7. The offender is not off the hook.

It's normal to think, *They've hurt me and now they get off scot-free?* And while it can feel that way, it's not truth. Choosing to forgive doesn't mean you're excusing that person for their offenses. It means you recognize that it's God who brings justice—not you.

Romans 12:19 says, "Again, my loved ones, do not seek revenge; instead, allow God's wrath to make sure justice is served. Turn it over to Him. For the Scriptures say, 'Revenge is Mine. I will settle all scores'" (voice). Oh yes, God will handle it. So take a deep breath. They're not off the hook; you're just off theirs.

8. Receiving an apology isn't necessary before you forgive.

Many of us have decided we'll forgive only if we receive an apology first. But that's so limiting. Think about it. What if you've lost contact with them or the offender was a stranger?

What if they've died? What if they don't even know they've hurt you? Waiting for someone to own their actions and words is a worthy hope but an unrealistic expectation.

If we're going to live out our one and only life in authentic ways, we can't be tangled by unforgiveness as we wait for someone to say *sorry*. Nope. Freedom will come when we decide to forgive anyway.

9. God commands that we forgive.

Have we forgotten this command? Too often we skip right over it because we think our current situation is too painful and God would understand our bitterness. But God tells us to forgive everyone—the betrayer, the murderer, the thief, the abuser, the liar. And honestly, this requires courage. But to be in a right relationship with our heavenly Father, we must obey Him—even His commands most difficult to obey. When we do, we're being authentic because we are doing what God created us to do. Love.

I know this was a hard list to work through. Thanks for sticking with me. Gosh, sometimes this whole forgiveness thing feels like a mountain too tall and steep to climb over. But when we sit with this list of benefits, we see why forgiveness is something God wants us to embrace.

We don't have to be afraid to extend grace, because there are legit reasons for it. And our willingness to forgive—with all the grit and grace we can muster—helps us shine into an offended world that needs to know there is a better way to live.

LEARNING TO FORGIVE YOURSELF

We may struggle to forgive ourselves the very most. Just what do we do when the one we need to give grace to is us?

Finding a way to forgive ourselves is tricky. And it may be the most destructive to our hearts if we let it fester for long. I appreciate that God included stories in the Bible about people who royally messed up and struggled to forgive themselves for falling short of their own standards or the standards others set for them. It helps me find grace for being terribly imperfect—for failing despite my best efforts. And it gives me courage to stop beating myself up for letting others down.

You know what else? It gives me permission to be myself. Because while God created me and delights in who I am, living a perfect life was never part of the plan. Neither was it for you.

Let's look at some characters from the Bible who needed to forgive themselves. These pillars of the faith struggled too! And pay close attention to God's response to their mistakes. Notice how their missteps didn't change how God saw them or disqualify them from their divinely appointed purpose. He was quick to forgive them.

And let's also note that they didn't allow their blunders to become their identity—at least not for long. I especially love that part. Rather than allow mistakes to define their true selves, they allowed their true selves to be defined by God. That takes courage and an encounter with the Healer.

In other words, they found the grit and grace to pursue an authentic life—a life lived as the person God intended them to be—instead of letting their failures and shortcomings take them out of the game altogether. Maybe knowing God forgave them was vital, but maybe finding the grace to forgive themselves was just as important.

PAUL (PREVIOUSLY SAUL)

If you remember, before he became the amazing Paul, Paul was the treacherous Saul. His goal was to destroy Christianity. He was on a mission to eradicate Christians once and for all, and he stopped at nothing to do it. He made these God-fearing men and women live in fear of his wrath, destroyed their churches, imprisoned them, and even murdered them. Yep, Saul was a first-class oppressor. This Jewish man was a crusader of hate until he had a life-changing encounter with Jesus.

In Acts 9, we learn that Saul had just gone to the high priest, asking for authorization to purge all the synagogues in Damascus of Jesus' followers. His hatred burned toward these people, and that loathing ignited his wrath. Once his request was granted, he set out on the journey.

Suddenly, he saw a flash of light and fell to the ground. Right there on the road to Damascus, a divine conversation took place.

Here is the exchange in verses 4–6 (VOICE):

> *The Lord: Saul, Saul, why are you attacking Me?*
> *Saul: Lord, who are You?*
> *The Lord: I am Jesus. I am the One you are attacking. Get up. Enter the city. You will learn there what you are to do.*

Back up the bus. Did you notice the instant forgiveness for Saul (soon to be Paul)? He was on his way to literally empty the temple and bring the Jesus-followers back to Jerusalem. And knowing his hatred for these people, we also know the process wouldn't be a civil one.

But there was a divine plan for Saul, and his unthinkable acts were completely forgiven by God—in that moment. He knew Saul was not living his authentic self, but instead was being manipulated by evil. He wasn't walking out the divine purpose for his life. He wasn't supposed to be a crusader for evil, but rather a crusader for good. And in that divine exchange, God got his attention and put him back on track.

Was Paul able to forgive himself? I believe so. In 1 Corinthians 15:9–10, he talked about how God brought out his true mission and purpose. "I'm the least of the apostles. I'm not even fit to be called an apostle because I persecuted God's church. But God's kindness *made me what I am*, and that kindness was not wasted on me" (NOG, emphasis mine). Forgiving himself was the only way he could wear the mantle God had for him. And Paul recognized his transformation and found the grit and grace to embrace it.

Only with God's help can we live our lives as our authentic selves.

DAVID

Yep, even this biblical rock star messed up and needed to embrace and extend forgiveness. This man after God's own heart made big mistakes that required heaps of grace. Gosh, I love this guy.

We first learn about David as a shepherd boy who defeated Goliath with a small stone and a big faith. And then we see his rocky ascension to the throne, eventually becoming the king of Israel. David is a central character in the Bible, and a beloved one too. No wonder God decided Jesus would descend from the House of David. What a beautiful gift of a powerful lineage. Without a doubt, David was loved and honored by His Creator.

But what you may not realize is that he was also the poster child for bad choices. The Bible shares many of his shortcomings, and among them are adultery (2 Samuel 11:4) and murder (2 Samuel 12:9). David didn't always make decisions that accurately reflected his authentic self, but God knew the truth of who David was.

What I admire the most about this character is his pursuit for authentic living. Even though his sins were many, he was quick to turn to God. He cried out and confessed his wretchedness. David was transparent and honest, always asking God for forgiveness. He realized his seasons of bad choices didn't define who God created him to be. And every time he cried out to his Creator, God forgave him. Every time.

Was David able to forgive himself? I think so. In 2 Samuel 12, it seems David comes to terms with the death of his son as punishment for his own misjudgment with Bathsheba. Once his child dies, he finds his resolve. He begins to eat again. He comforts his wife. And rather than continue to beat himself up, it appears David steps into his identity as the king and a worshipper and once again pursues living his life as God ordained.

MOSES

Oh Moses. Yes, even this great man of God who walked the Israelites out of their four-hundred-year slavery stint in Egypt messed up and needed forgiveness. Girl, we are in good company!

Did you know this kindhearted, insecure man was also a murderer? While still living as an Egyptian in Pharaoh's house, he killed a taskmaster he saw beating a Hebrew worker in the field. At this point, he knew his true identity was with the Hebrew people, so watching this injustice was too much for Moses. Here's what happened:

> [Moses] *witnessed an Egyptian beating one of his Hebrew brothers. He looked around to see if anyone was watching but there was no one in sight, so he beat the Egyptian just as the Egyptian had beaten the Hebrew. Moses ended up killing the Egyptian and hid the dead body in the sand.* (Exodus 2:11–12 VOICE)

It may have been righteous anger that rose up in him, but murder is murder. And rather than stay and face consequences, he ran. Moses left Egypt behind in hopes of starting a new life. But regardless of all these bad choices, God forgave him. Even more, He knew the authentic Moses—the one He created—and God *still* used him to lead two million Israelites out of slavery and into freedom.

I dug around for any scripture that mentions Moses' ability to extend grace to himself, but I couldn't find any. But here are my personal thoughts. When God first called Moses to march back into Egypt and command Pharaoh to release His people, maybe part of the reason Moses was hesitant and insecure was because he felt unworthy. He had remembered all his shortcomings. And so Moses was unable to accept the call from God with confidence because he wasn't able to see himself the way God saw him.

But his time in the wilderness with the Israelites looked different. I noticed that when Moses came down from the mountain carrying the Ten Commandments after forty days, he seemed to have a newfound acceptance and authority in the role God placed him in. I think he and God did some serious business up on that mountain, and I imagine it included self-forgiveness for times and places he fell short of expectations. How could it not?

When we harbor an unwillingness to forgive ourselves, it shakes our confidence. And a lack of confidence keeps us from seeing who we really are. It keeps us from living authentic with ourselves and others because we're ashamed.

Now, I've only scratched the surface with Bible characters. You could dig deeper by looking at the stories of Tamar, Peter, Jonah, and just about anyone else mentioned in God's Word. Every one of them needed to experience forgiveness on some level— from God, from others, or from themselves. And a few even needed a swift kick in the pants to start functioning in their authenticity.

LEARNING TO FORGIVE GOD

Now, this may sound weird, but I'm giving you permission to be angry with God if that's how you're feeling today. Sometimes we forget God can handle every single bit of us—even the ugly parts. He can handle all your pain, all your sadness, and all the rage and resentment you may be harboring toward Him. God sees your hurt and knows how you're justifying your unwillingness to forgive Him. And because of God's love for you and His care for details you're struggling with, He is waiting for you to reach out to Him.

You know what? I've been spittin' mad at God plenty of times. He's permitted situations that have knocked me to my knees and broken my heart. Evil has barreled its way into my world and turned it upside down more than once.

And God has allowed some mean-spirited people to speak hateful words and do hurtful things that crushed my spirit. Oh, I know your life hasn't been a cakewalk either. Whose life has been, right?

So how do we forgive God when it feels like He's let us down? How do we move past feelings of betrayal by our heavenly Father, wondering why He didn't show up when we needed Him the most?

The truth is we expect God to have our back since we're His children. Because we're His prized creations, we assume He'll act like a helicopter parent and hover over us so life works in our favor. Sometimes we think that because we're saved, life should be easy. And if not easy, then at least easier than most. And when we get sucker punched in the gut, we cry out to God. *Where were You? Why didn't You? How could You?*

Betrayal is a deep wound, and I'm sending you a hug right now. Friend, if you're feeling like God has turned His back on you or let you down, I get you. I've been to that same place, felt those same emotions, and it caused great distance between me and my heavenly Father.

While I didn't realize it at the time, being sexually abused by a stranger at the age of four left me with huge betrayal issues as an adult. I questioned where God was and why He allowed that life-changing-event-for-the-worse to happen to someone He claimed in His Word to love—an innocent child, for Pete's sake! And in my pain, I ran in the opposite direction from God. For years.

Now, my situation was hard and horrible and has taken years to overcome, but it's nothing compared to what Job experienced. I'm not trying to minimize my abuse or its effects, but what I went through pales in comparison to what this

Bible character had to weather. Let's visit the story of Job.

The opening verse of his self-titled book reads, "He was a very good man—his character spotless, his integrity unquestioned. In fact, he so believed in God that he sought to honor Him in all things. He deliberately avoided evil in all of his affairs" (Job 1:1 VOICE). In other words, Job was completely legit and 100 percent sold out for God.

Maybe it's just me, but if I was this amazing in the eyes of God, I might think *my* goodness should warrant *His* goodness. Know what I mean? I might begin thinking that because I was doing such a stellar job of walking the line, God would have my back and shelter me from harm. But that couldn't have been further from the truth.

In a conversation between the Enemy and God, Job's name came up. The Lord mentioned what a righteous man he was, and then He gave permission for Satan to go after Job. Wait. What? The only condition was that Job's life be spared. I encourage you to read chapter 1 of Job to see the exchange between these two superpowers. It's almost unbelievable.

As Satan descended on Job, all hell literally broke loose. And in the end, four different messengers confronted Job with horrible news. With God's permission, here's what the Enemy did to this upright man, by the numbers:

- One thousand donkeys and oxen were stolen by the Sabeans.
  - ⋆ All but one servant with the livestock were killed (messenger #1) .

- Seven thousand sheep were killed by lightning.
  - ⋆ All but one shepherd with the sheep were killed (messenger #2).

- Three thousand camels were stolen by the Chaldeans.
  - ★ All but one servant with the camels were killed (messenger #3).
- All seven sons and all three daughters were killed when the house collapsed on them.
  - ★ All but one partying with them were killed (messenger #4).

I cannot begin to fathom the pain in Job's heart. And all this heartache happened within one day. Job had enjoyed such prosperity and favor, and then God allowed it all to be ripped away. He allowed Job to be tested. Whoa, talk about feelings of betrayal.

Deep breath. Even with all this calamity, God remained good. This is undeniable truth even if it feels unfathomable at times. You see, God authorized the stripping of Job's possessions and family *only* because it would ultimately benefit our main character and glorify Himself.

He isn't a reckless God. He isn't a thoughtless God. Nor is He a heartless one. Second Corinthians 4:15 confirms this truth. It reads, "All of this is happening *for your good*. As grace is spread to the multitudes, there is a growing sound of thanks being uttered by those relishing in the glory of God" (VOICE, emphasis mine).

A lot of misguided and frustrating discussions between friends take place in the next several chapters. You'll want to make sure to spend some time reading through them. But in the interest of getting to my final point, I'm going to highlight the progress: Job deeply mourns and grieves his loss, his friends try to help but are full of bad theology, his wife shows no support, and Job's confidence in God's love for him begins to waver.

And then Job begins to complain to God. In chapter 38, the Lord responds by asking him questions, calling Job out. God's words in the section are directed right at our main character. Since His set of questions back to Job are so long, I'm sharing only a sampling. Buckle up.

> *Where were you when I dug and laid the foundation of the earth? Explain it to me, if you are acquainted with understanding. Who decided on the measurements? Surely you know that! Who stretched out a line to measure the dimensions? Upon what base was the foundation set? Or who laid the cornerstone on the day when the stars of the morning broke out in song and God's heavenly throng, elated, shouted along?* (vv. 4–7 VOICE)

> *In your short run of days, have you ever commanded the morning to begin or taught the sun to rise in its place? Under your watch has the early light ever taken hold of the earth by the edges and shaken the wicked loose?* (vv. 12–13 VOICE)

> *Can you bellow out orders at the clouds and pull down a flood of rain around you? Can you dispatch bolts of lightning on their way, who instantly* obey *and* say *to you, "Here we are"?* (vv. 34–35 VOICE)

And, friend, this goes on from chapter 38 through chapter 41. Honestly, my heart goes out to Job. I can't even imagine. I'd be freaking out listening to God lay out His reasons for why my questions weren't warranted or appropriate. I'd be overwhelmed listening to God's responses. This interrogation must have left Job without words and trembling with fear. Then in chapter 42, Job speaks.

> *Before I knew only what I had heard of You, but now I have seen You. Therefore I realize the truth; I disavow and mourn all I have said and repent in dust and ash.* (vv. 5–6 voice)

Job backed up the bus. He renounced his complaining. He recanted his questioning of God. Instead, He chose to recognize that God was God. . .and he was not. He chose to trust that if God did what He did—or allowed what He allowed—it was all for His glory and Job's benefit. In that moment, any anger Job had toward God was gone. And he forgave Him—not for God's benefit, but for his own. He needed to let go of the idea that God had done wrong toward him, even though God's actions had allowed such pain.

Job didn't have to have all the answers. They weren't necessary. And demanding answers from God is unrealistic and inappropriate because we don't get to know them. We're not God. This is a tough truth, I know. And it's a hard reality to grab onto when we feel betrayed and want to understand the *whys*. But from one sister to another, please hear my heart. Trusting God helps us forgive Him when it *feels* like He's abandoned us. He never will abandon us, but it can feel that way.

From Job's story, we can find five truths that make forgiving God something we can muster the grit and grace to do:

1. You'll never fully understand God's will or ways. We must come to *know* this.

2. God doesn't make mistakes. We must come to *accept* this.
3. God is sovereign. We must come to *believe* this.
4. God is good all the time. We must come to *trust* this.
5. God is for you in every way. We must come to *recognize* this.

Only God—*only God*—can be completely trustworthy in His motives. Only God always wants the best for us (which isn't always the same as what we want). Only God has a perfect track record in our lives. Yep, only God.

Part of having faith means we believe God is who He says He is. And that faith allows us to choose to forgive Him. It means we stop being angry with Him. We stop being resentful. We release what we believe to be offenses we're holding against Him. And just like Job, we know who our real enemy is. Forgiving—accepting his plan—is a choice we must make.

There's no easy fix for forgiveness, but the ability is baked into each of us. It's part of our original DNA, our identity, our true selves. And this is where we need grit and grace to kick in so we can work through unforgiveness and live the authentic life we were created to live.

Take a minute to think about who you need to forgive. Whose hurtful actions are consuming your thoughts? Who do you want to get even with? Whose painful words do you continue to ruminate on day after day after day? What painful event are you still stuck on?

Let today be the day all that changes.

I wrote this forgiveness declaration for me. But something tells me you could use it too. I'll be honest: sometimes

I'm clenching my teeth as I work through it. Forgiveness is hard. Other times I'm in tears as I write it out. Regardless, this is a powerful tool to store in your authentic-living arsenal.

You may want to write this in your journal or type it out on your computer. You can print the statement and keep it in a folder—whatever makes the most sense to you.

FORGIVENESS DECLARATION

Today __/__/__, I am choosing to forgive _____ for _____ _____ _____.

In my pain, what I'd like to do or have already done is: (circle the ones that apply)

retaliate	gossip	play victim
humiliate	punish	embarrass
ruminate	hold on to	spread rumors
give silent	offense	give a taste of own
treatment	entertain hate	medicine
hide away	recruit an army	

But I know these responses to my pain are not God's heart for me. I was created to forgive because I was created in the image of God.

I know this is a process and I'm human. So I promise to give myself grace when I need to revisit this declaration and re-forgive my offender. Sometimes it's not a once-and-done process.

Because I don't want anything to hinder my ability to live an authentic life, I am committed to seeking freedom rather than sitting in the bondage of my pain.

I am fully aware that. . .

_____ forgiving doesn't mean I must forget the offense.

_____ forgiving doesn't let the offender off the hook for hurting me.

_____ I don't need an apology to forgive.

_____ forgiving doesn't mean I won't feel the pain.

_____ forgiving is for my benefit first and foremost.

_____ it's often appropriate to set up healthy boundaries, if necessary.

I also recognize that. . .

_____ healing is a beautiful by-product of forgiveness.

_____ God commands us to forgive.

_____ forgiveness often requires divine intervention.

My Prayer

God, please honor my heart! I am trying hard to forgive offense(s) that are threatening my ability to live the way You created me to live. Honestly, I'm afraid to forgive because I'm afraid it will invalidate my pain. But I'm learning that's not truth. Help me remember that forgiveness is not to benefit the one who hurt me, but instead to benefit me. That can feel so counterintuitive, but Your economy runs by a different set of rules. So, would You give me the grit to extend grace quickly and fully? And would You bless my desire to live an authentic life with myself, others, and You? Praise You, Father. In Jesus' name, amen.

Here's the beauty of this declaration. You can revisit and re-use it anytime, no matter the situation. Let this be a tool to help you walk out forgiveness in your everyday life, thriving as the person God created you to be.

Your greatest tool, however, is God Himself. It's His Holy Spirit in you that ignites the desire and ability to let go of offenses. In your own strength, you may fail. You can pretend to be okay for only so long before the hidden unforgiveness begins to leak out in unhealthy ways. And sometimes we need a trusted friend or counselor to help us navigate the process. Don't be afraid to embrace help.

Let's extend and embrace forgiveness so nothing hinders our ability to live authentic lives pleasing to God. It's an everyday choice you and I get to make.

FINDING THE GRIT

What does unforgiveness look like in your life?

How does it change how you live and love others?

How have you tried to justify the unforgiveness you're holding on to?

How would your life be different if you chose to extend grace?

What did God speak to you through this chapter?

How does forgiveness help you live authentic?

Finding the Grace

Father, forgiveness is so hard! Honestly, sometimes I just don't want to do it for a million different reasons. But I know You have commanded us to extend grace to everyone and in every situation. I know that forgiveness is for my benefit. And I know that it's Your Holy Spirit in me that will help me release offenses. Would You show me how to be a woman full of grace? Would You help me love others well? I want to be a light for You by living an authentic life. Please give me the grit and grace to embrace forgiveness so I can shine. In Jesus' mighty name I pray, amen.

Live
Accept Your Awesomeness
Unearth the Untruths
Try Loving Everyone
Hold on to Hope
Embrace and Extend Forgiveness
N
T
I
C

CHAPTER 9

Never Shrink Back

Our greatest weakness lies in giving up. The most certain
way to succeed is always to try just one more time.
—Thomas Edison[12]

*J*didn't see the post on my Facebook wall for over an
hour. Only when I opened the private message sent to me,
berating my heart with mean-spirited and misguided words,
did I even get a hint that something was wrong.

"You're classless for calling out a ministry peer in your
video. Shame on you, Carey. I thought you were better than
that." This comment hit me right in the gut. The attack
seemed to come out of nowhere, and I was struggling to get
my footing again. *What had I done? What was I missing?*

The video referenced was the promotional video for my
last book. In it, I shared a story of being unfriended in real
life by someone I thought was a good friend. Of course, no
names were mentioned. All details were changed. There was
absolutely no way anyone could figure out who I was talking

about. That wasn't even the point to begin with.

Honestly, someone would have to try really hard to find offense in that video. The focus wasn't on the person who hurt my feelings, but on the challenge to respond in uncommon ways when we get hurt. It was encouragement to live differently in a world so bent toward offense.

Shame has been a huge tangle God and I have been loosening, but this tightened it. Insecurities began flooding in. Even worse, this was launch day for my book *Uncommon*, and my Facebook wall was busier than normal. I deleted the message and then sat with the Lord, asking for insight.

Looking back now, it makes me laugh. Someone got offended by a video suggesting we not get offended so easily.

Maybe you can relate to this kind of situation because you've been told to keep quiet. You've been told to ignore something wrong. You've been called out for being honest. You've felt the pull to back down so you wouldn't cause waves. Sometimes people want us to pretend everything is just fine—even when it's not at all. They want us to hide our stories so no one feels uncomfortable. But when we agree to shrink away from our truth, we're choosing counterfeit living.

But you know what? This story is my story, which means I get to share it if I choose. And when we tell our stories in appropriate ways, they can become powerful ministry tools. Our testimonies can connect with hearts in profound ways and change someone's life. They can offer courage and strengthen resolve. It's okay to be real and honest. If we're being respectful and letting God be the hero of the story, we should never shrink back from sharing our experiences.

My private message back to this person was short and to

the point. "This is my story, and I get to tell it." I didn't lash out. (Oh, I wanted to.) I didn't crumble under insecurity. I held true to who I am. And I refused to let shame whisper lies into my heart.

We're alive at such an interesting time, aren't we? So often, I feel honored that God chose to bring me onto the Kingdom calendar in today's wacky world. I love that He trusts me to speak truth and life, here and now. But I'll be honest. Sometimes this place totally freaks me out and makes me want to tuck myself away from all the crazy. I want to keep quiet rather than speak out. I want to fly under the radar and just do my own thing. I want to go with the flow rather than cause ripples. And sometimes I'd rather be agreeable instead of authentic.

It takes real courage—real grit and grace—to be yourself, especially when yourself is a Jesus-girl. These days that doesn't always go over very well. And while we may want to pull back because we're afraid of being ridiculed, now is the perfect time to stand firm in who we are. We can't back down from doing what God has called us to do. The world needs Jesus now.

A few years ago, I might have let that person get away with being rude about the content of my video. I probably wouldn't have had the gumption to advocate for myself. I would have let it taint my mood. I may have played the victim, talking it through with others. And I would have replayed the exchange over and over in my own mind, trying to make sense of it. But not anymore.

Now, I'm not suggesting you attend every fight you're invited to, but let's not shrink back in situations that warrant our steadfastness.

I'm proud of who I am. Listen, God and I have worked hard to heal some very broken places. And I take His call on my life seriously. I want that for you too. We don't have time to shrink back in fear. It's time to stand up for what we believe in. It's time to stand with confidence in who God created us to be. We certainly aren't perfect, but we have great purpose here on planet Earth. Both of us. All of us.

Think about the changes we've seen in our nation's relationship with God over the past several years. As Christ-followers, we're getting pushback as we try to live our faith out loud. We're being told to keep God tucked away until we're in the privacy of our own homes. People get offended when we wear shirts or jewelry with a Christian message. The powers that be are trying to remove God from our currency and our government buildings. They're trying to stop prayers on football fields, remove God's name from the Pledge of Allegiance, and change "Merry Christmas" to "Happy holidays." And many of us are staying silent as they march forward with their agenda. We're shrinking back because it feels easier. It feels safer.

I know being real about our faith is scary, but we are God's army on earth. You and I are the hands and feet of Jesus. We are salt and light. We are His plan A for spreading the Gospel to the lost. We're the ones whose words and actions are supposed to point others to our Father in heaven. Friend, we cannot shy away from being ourselves. You see, God baked something right into you and me that we're to share with the world. We cannot hide our faith, because we weren't made to do so. And when we ask for Him to do so, God will give us the grit and grace to be who He created us to be.

Here is some sobering truth. If we choose not to be real about the ways God intersects with our lives, we'll miss the opportunity to encourage someone. If we don't share our testimonies with others who need to know hope still exists, hope will die. If we're not letting our words and actions shine Jesus, we're missing the point of our existence. Scared or not, we just can't shrink back from authenticity. Our community needs to know there is a better way.

PAUL

Paul paints a beautiful picture of what it means to be confident in God and stay true to ourselves in Romans 1:16. "For I am *not the least bit embarrassed* about the gospel. I won't shy away from it, because it is God's power to save every person who believes: first the Jew, and then the non-Jew" (VOICE, emphasis mine).

When Paul wrote this, he was about to preach in Rome. This great world-center was full of all sorts of peoples, many unfamiliar with the Gospel and most open to perversions of all kinds. It lacked a moral backbone and celebrated anything and everything under the sun. Sounds a little familiar, doesn't it? Paul was walking into a situation that most of us would shy away from.

Under the reign of Nero, Rome was a heathen's happy place. It's true that Paul was bold, but if there was anywhere he'd struggle to talk about Jesus, it would be here. Yet his statement in Romans 1:16 is power-packed with grit and grace. He was making a conscious choice to be intrepid, and he was unashamed to be himself and share his Savior.

On that road to Damascus, an encounter with God turned him from a murderer to a missionary. And nothing would make him back down from spreading the Word of God among gentile nations. What a beautiful example of courage to live authentic in counterfeit situations where we may be in the minority.

NOAH

And then there's Noah. In Genesis 6, we learn how frustrated and heartbroken God was over the state of the world. Verse 5 reads, "The Eternal One saw that wickedness was rampaging throughout the earth and that evil had become the first thought on every mind" (VOICE). Again, doesn't that sound familiar to the state of our nation and world right now? In His divine frustration, God decided to wipe out humanity. Scripture tells us that in that moment, He grieved His creation.

But then in verse 8 we see His dilemma. "But there was one person whom the Lord could not let go of—Noah— because this man pleased Him" (VOICE). According to verse 9, Noah was a good man, a righteous man, and the "best man of his generation" (VOICE). Even more, he had a close relationship with God.

Don't miss that in a crazy world where evil reigned, Noah stayed true to himself and his Creator. He didn't join in. He lived authentic—lived the way God created Him to live. And as we all know, that's no easy feat. Just like David, he found the courage to stand up against so much evil. And God noticed.

The Lord downloaded the building plans and then made a covenant agreement with Noah. "To survive, you and your family—you, your wife, your sons, and your sons' wives— must go into the ark" (v. 18 VOICE). Think about the criticism

Noah and his family must have endured from the community during the construction. The massive boat sitting on dry land was certainly fodder for haters. But this righteous man persevered, listening to God. It didn't bother him to appear foolish, because he knew he wasn't foolish at all. He was obedient. Noah was being his authentic self by doing what God created him to do. And the Lord honored his worthy pursuit by saving him and his family.

Noah reminds us that our authenticity isn't always understood by others. It may seem silly or prudish or flat-out wrong to them. But when God thought us up, He designed plans for our lives—plans that require us to be true to how He made us. Let's not shrink back, but instead trust God for the grit and grace to be our genuine selves.

DAVID

My all-time favorite story about being unashamedly bold is when David stands up to Goliath. I am clinging to this story right now. I'm facing down a huge giant, and this story gives me grit. And hope. I'd like to spend a little time unpacking this story in more detail, because chances are you're facing your own Goliath. And while you may have heard this account a million times, I'm hoping God will reveal a fresh, new detail to encourage your weary heart. Sound good?

In 1 Samuel 17, the Philistine and Israelite armies were gathered on opposite hilltops for battle in a valley between them. As preparations got under way, a fearsome giant named Goliath stepped out of the Philistine camp and into the spotlight.

- Goliath was over nine feet tall.
- He had pristine armor from head to toe.
- His chain-mail coat weighed over one hundred pounds.
- His spear shaft alone was between 2 and 2.5 inches in diameter.
- The head of his spear weighed close to twenty pounds.

Goliath was also highly trained and carried the title of *champion*. He was cocky too, assured of his abilities because of his strength and size. Scripture tells us he taunted the Israelites verbally for forty days, but just the sight of this giant scared them. Not one Israelite soldier was willing to step out and fight the behemoth.

And then David showed up.

This is David before he was *the* King David. He's just a teenager who cared for the family's livestock back home, and his father has sent him to the battlefield to take food and check on his older brothers, who were part of the Israelite army. But when David saw this giant and heard his sneers and jeers toward his countrymen, he volunteered. David mustered the grit and grace to fight Goliath.

Now, time out. What did David know that the others didn't? The only battle experiences this kid had was fighting off bears and lions, and now he was ready to take on the likes of this champion? Friend, this is grit on steroids. This is crazy courage. David was the underdog taking on a favored warrior who had everything going for him. But this kid knew who he was and who God is. And he believed in both.

Sometimes we just decide enough is enough. I feel that right now in my situation. I've been bullied long enough by the Goliath in front of me. It has taunted and chastised me ruthlessly. And while this giant may appear bigger and better, it's not. I may not be able to take down this Goliath on my own, but my God is bigger than anything that comes against me. Truth like this ignites my courage to stare back at challenges with resolve. And when I stand in His strength, I'm being authentic, because I know where my true power and might come from. I'm unafraid to battle.

Can you just imagine the naysayers bantering back and forth as David bent down and chose five smooth stones from the stream? Think about those still on the hilltops—probably in both camps—laughing at the misguided gumption of this teenager. But none of it fazed David. He was unafraid. Nothing would make him shrink back, and he was about to shine.

With his staff in one hand and his slingshot in the other, he marched toward the battlefield. In your mind's eye, can you see the grit in David's eyes? Can you see his confidence? Oh yes, David knew who he was, and he knew God would give him strength and favor to kill his enemy. There was no shred of doubt. And then he spoke to the giant:

You come to me carrying a sword and spear and javelin as your weapons, but I come armed with the name of the Eternal One, the Commander of heavenly armies, the True God of the armies of Israel, the One you have insulted. *This very day, the Eternal One will give you into my hands. I will strike you down and cut off your head, and I will feed the birds of the air and the wild animals*

of the fields with the flesh of your Philistine warriors.
Then all the land will know the True God is with Israel,
and all of those gathered here will know that the Eternal
One does not save by sword and spear. The battle is the
Eternal One's, and He will give you into our hands.
(1 Samuel 17:45–47 VOICE, emphasis mine)

Whoa. David didn't shrink back—not even a little. This was bold confidence, and I admire his unwavering trust in God. This is proof positive that your age doesn't matter. Whether you're a teenager, in your golden years, or somewhere in between, you can find the confidence in God you need to stand your ground.

David called Goliath out for insulting God, and right now we're watching our society do the same thing Goliath did. Be it our neighbors, coworkers, friends and family, actors in television and movies, or politicians, it feels like everyone is taking God's holy name in vain. They curse Him with their careless words. They call God a myth or an outdated story. They refuse to acknowledge His power and authority, and we're sitting by, watching it happen without saying a thing.

In our fear of putting ourselves out there, sometimes we stay silent rather than stand up and respond with truth. We often shrink back instead. But that's not who God created us to be. Our silence is unacceptable. We weren't created to shy away in fear or apathy. And while we shouldn't be mean or rude or disrespectable with our words, we can be honest.

David wasn't okay with Goliath insulting God, and rather than let it go, he pointed it out. He didn't shrink back from addressing it. David was being his authentic self by standing up for what he knew was right. He was being authentic by doing what God called him to do. His authenticity was proven through his belief that God would do what He said He would do. Yep, David chose to be real with how he lived his life. It wasn't always pretty, and he messed up an awful lot, but his pursuit of being who God made him to be is noteworthy.

Think about it. Paul walked into Rome unafraid. Noah continued to follow God when he was literally the last righteous person on earth. And now we see David standing up for God and his community, risking his life. Friend, where is your courage to be who the Lord created you to be? Where are you missing the opportunity to shine Jesus into the world? Why aren't you being your authentic self to those who need to see an example of a godly woman?

Let's see how this story ends. Scripture tells us David ran toward the giant, reached into his bag, placed a stone in his sling, and sent the stone flying toward his adversary. As it sank deep into the Philistine's forehead, it brought him down hard. Then David picked up Goliath's own sword and cut off his head. His death set into motion victory for the Israelite army.

I love everything about this story. David's grit was a result of his confidence in God. And this account proves that if we have that same attitude, we'll find the courage we need to stand up against any giant that comes our way. We don't have to shrink back in fear. We can ask God for the grit and grace to be who He created us to be.

A friend once said this to me: "I don't want to be bold, because it makes me look prideful and pushy." I was encouraging her to stand up for herself in a tough situation that left her feeling weak. Her fear was that others might consider her courage a misguided attempt for control. She worried that speaking up might make her look too demanding or manipulative. My friend didn't want to come off as mean-spirited in her honesty.

I think there may be some wisdom in that. It's not the best strategy to collide with the world, insisting others do what we say. We can't say unkind things in unkind ways, hiding behind a banner of honesty. Steamrolling isn't the most effective way to get someone's attention. We don't want to incite anger or point fingers. And acting in these ways isn't being our true self, nor is it being a light to others.

But deep down, the unwillingness to share her thoughts was rooted in fear. She was afraid of offending someone or being criticized. She didn't feel worthy of speaking up, advocating for her needs. And in the end, she opted to stay quiet. This amazing woman is facing those same giants today and is still cowering like the Israelite army. She just can't find her gumption to share those deep concerns with others. Are we guilty of doing the same thing?

Choosing to be bold is risky when we rely on our own strength. But like Paul and Noah and David, when our courage is rooted in God, we can stand firm without letting fear take over. We can be real without being rude.

Several years ago I was on a safari in South Africa—a dream come true. Being an animal lover, I was giddy at the opportunity to see lions, elephants, hippos, and giraffes live and in Technicolor. It was mind-blowing. We drove through the preserve in jeeps, and I soaked in every bit of information our guides shared. It was a once-in-a-lifetime experience.

As we arrived back at home base, I noticed an enclosure

with two cheetahs. A few people were in and around the area, so I got out of the jeep and walked over. An employee was sharing how these two cats had been abandoned by their mother at birth. Until they were ready to live successfully on their own, the preserve was committed to raising them. The cheetahs were less than a year old but the size of adults. And beautiful.

When he offered to let me go inside the enclosure and pet the animals, I jumped at the opportunity. It never even crossed my mind to be fearful. Of all the animals on God's green earth, I love cats. All kinds. All sizes. From domesticated to wild. I love their power. I love their independence. I love their unpredictability. I went inside without a second thought.

Once in, I bent down on one knee to pet a cheetah lounging on its side. Being right next to this huge cat was surreal, breathtaking. And as I began to rub my hand up and down its backbone, the cheetah started purring. Its fur felt greasy and dirty, but there was no way I was going to stop. I was in heaven.

Within a few minutes, the other cheetah started to walk over to me. He rubbed against me as he passed, and that slight graze pushed me forward. This cat's power was notable and impressive. As he lay down, I began petting him too. What I wanted to do was curl up with these two lovebugs and kiss all over their faces, but I knew better. And after about thirty minutes, the man with me in the enclosure said it was time to leave.

I stood up, turned, and started walking toward the gate. With my back to the cats, I was unable to see them, but one got up and started toward me—quickly. The man grabbed my hand, whipped me around, and told me to stand tall and look the cat right in the eyes. Immediately. He said, "Never turn your back on these cats. Don't shrink into a submissive role. Stand bold and let them know you're a force to be reckoned with. If you don't show them who you are, they will kill you." And when I did, the cat veered off and laid back down.

Sometimes when I tell this story, I like to embellish it by saying I had a near-death experience with a cheetah on the plains of Africa. I know I'm bent toward drama because that makes for a better story. But in all honesty, I believe the cat recognized a gap in authority and was poised to take a stand. I don't know if it would have attacked me, but it saw my vulnerability as an opportunity.

Here's what I learned from that experience. One of our greatest weapons against counterfeit living is showing the world who we really are. If we choose to shrink back, be silent, or turn a blind eye, we dishonor the God who created us, we let down the community depending on us, and we fall short of the calling placed on our lives.

Shrinking back sounds like this:

I am so insecure and afraid to be real because I'm pretty sure they won't like what I have to say. It's just not worth the risk.

There is nothing special about me. No one listens to what I have to say. So it really doesn't matter if I'm courageous or not.

I think it's better to hide my faith so no one gets offended.

These are real comments from real women. And while they feel like justification to the one speaking them, they aren't. These words are spoken from a place of fear and insecurity. Saying them helps the women rationalize their inaction, but they're missing the point. Their authentic selves are gifts to the world, even in their glorious imperfections and divine complexities. If we choose not to be the *real* us—not do the work God designed for us to do or be the people He created us to be—it changes things.

Think about it. If Paul hadn't shared the Gospel with gentiles, where would we be now? If Noah had refused to build the ark, would there be anyone alive today? If David hadn't volunteered to fight the giant, what would have become of the man after God's own heart? Sister, you are not weak. Your past does not disqualify you. And the goal for your life isn't to be loved and accepted. It's to obey God and shine the light He has placed in you. . .to the world.

How can we do this? Here's how:

For I can do everything God asks me to with the help of Christ who gives me the strength and power.
(Philippians 4:13 TLB)

So what should we say about all of this? If God is on our side, then tell me: whom should we fear?
(Romans 8:31 VOICE)

For the Eternal is always there to protect you.
He will safeguard your each and every step.
(Proverbs 3:26 VOICE)

Who do you think gave Paul, Noah, and David the grit and grace to do the task God called them to? Who gave them the strength and knowledge? Where did they get the courage to be themselves? Sometimes we think God calls only those who are fully confident and prepared. But that couldn't be further from the truth. God doesn't call the equipped; he equips the called. Rather than shrink back, we need to believe that He will give us what we need to walk out the call.

My job—*your job*—is to say yes to the Lord.

You may think you need to clean up your life first. You may feel like you need to get more experience under your belt. You might even think you're not strong enough or smart enough or holy enough to do God's work. And because of that, shrinking back feels better. But God is in the business of calling the ordinary into service. All throughout the Bible, you see examples of flawed people being used to do amazing things.

- Noah was a drunk.
- Abraham was old.
- Jacob was a liar.
- Leah was unattractive.
- Joseph was rejected by his jealous brothers.
- Moses stuttered and lacked confidence.
- Gideon was a scaredy-cat.
- Sampson was a womanizer.
- Rahab was a prostitute.
- Jeremiah and Timothy were young.
- David had an affair and was a murderer.
- Elijah had suicidal thoughts.
- Isaiah preached without clothes on.
- Jonah ran from God.
- Naomi was a widow.
- Job went bankrupt and lost almost everything.
- John the Baptist ate bugs.
- Peter denied Christ three times.

- The disciples fell asleep while praying.
- Martha was a worrywart.
- The Samaritan woman had been divorced several times.
- Zacchaeus was too short.
- Paul was too religious.
- Timothy had stomach issues.

Every one of these characters could have said no. They could have hidden away rather than finding the grit and grace to be authentic! But I love that they didn't. Their yes may not always have been immediate, but they eventually stood in the confidence that God made them for good works

They were a mixture of messy, crazy, insecure, eclectic, unpopular, and scandalous men and women who refused to let fear keep them from service. Knowing that this motley crew didn't shrink back, what's your excuse?

You can always find reasons to tuck yourself away, but that's not who you are. You're not a coward. You're not a fake. And while you may not be perfect, you can be purposeful to live an authentic life that points to our Father in heaven.

And, friend, I'll be right there on the battlefield with you. Together we can do this.

FINDING THE GRIT

What kind of courage did your family model as you were growing up?

What keeps you from being bold?

How did the stories of David, Noah, and Paul encourage you? What is your next right step?

What difference would it make if you chose to be courageous rather than shrink back in your faith?

What did God speak to you through this chapter?

How does being bold help you live authentic?

Finding the Grace

Father, I confess that sometimes I shrink back from living boldly in my faith. I know You created me to be a light, but it can be exhausting and scary. Remind me that in those overwhelming times, I need to ask for Your strength to help me stand firm in the truth. I want to be like Paul and Noah and David. They faced harsh communities unaccepting of You and still shined their true selves into their communities. Our world really isn't that much different. It's still full of people who need to know life can be different when we say yes to a relationship with Jesus. I want to be unashamed to be myself. I want to be confident in how You created me. Would You please help me find the grit and grace to be unafraid to live an authentic life? I just cannot do this without You. In Jesus' mighty name I pray, amen.

Live
Accept Your Awesomeness
Unearth the Untruths
Try Loving Everyone
Hold on to Hope
Embrace and Extend Forgiveness
Never Shrink Back
T
I
C

CHAPTER 10

Trample the Negatives

Being positive does not mean ignoring the negative.
Being positive means overcoming the negative.
Ralph Marston[13]

I'll be honest, negative people have a way of sucking the life right out of me. And self-preservation makes me avoid cynical people like the plague. Life is hard enough, and it brings me down to listen to someone who is *always* pessimistic. It's like sandpaper on my skin.

Now, I'm not totally devoid of grace. I know it's one thing to be down all the time and quite another to be walking through a tough season or situation. There is so much grace for that. We all need our community to rally around us as we navigate hard times. We need people with whom we can be authentic—sharing the nitty-gritty heart issues. But when someone is always in crisis, moving from one negative to the next in an endless cycle, it becomes a problem for me. It's overusing their authenticity. Instead of allowing God to bring a healthy understanding and perspective, they vomit their endless mess onto everyone. And they decide it's okay because they are *just being real*.

Sometimes I want to say, "Enough already. Find the good. There is always something good!" It is possible to find good in the bad. We can find positives in the negatives. And when we muster the grit to hold on to Jesus, letting Him be our hope, we can navigate the hard seasons with expectation and faith. This ability is baked into us. It's accessible through God's help. And it's part of our authentic self.

The truth is that happy people are more fun to be around. Their optimism reminds us that, among the messy, there is goodness in the world. We watch them traverse heartaches, and it gives us courage for our own journey. We see their steadfast trust in God, and it offers us confidence to face our giants. And they're the kind of people I want to be around the most. I deeply appreciate the company of overcomers.

Just this morning, I heard from someone I deeply admire that she's been diagnosed with breast cancer. She's had a heck of a few years already, and now this. As I sat stunned and saddened by the news, wondering why God would have allowed cancer to pile on her during this messy season of life, she didn't. Rather than share the news in tears, she talked about how much she trusted God. Instead of complaining that she had one more mountain to climb, she encouraged those around her through scripture. This sweet woman trampled the negatives by showing us her authentic faith. I want to be like *that*.

But if I were honest, I'd admit sometimes I wear that Negative Nelly name tag with conviction. I can throw a pity party with the best of them. Sometimes life feels so big and overwhelming that I can't see past the hurt and frustration. And rather than find the silver lining, I locate the remote control, grab some yogurt pretzels, and find yummy blankets to burrow into. Instead of speaking out God's promises, I speak out discouragement and hopelessness. I sit in defeat, moaning and groaning. And it not only feels good; it feels justified.

Like when my five-feet-ten-inches tall, freshman-varsity-volleyball-playing daughter sits on the bench rather than plays in the game she loves. Or when my son's multiyear crush decides not to talk to him anymore and it breaks his heart into a million pieces. Or when my husband's boss gets mad because Wayne stood up for truth and he goes from king-of-the-hill to run-of-the-mill overnight. Or when someone makes a comment that cuts right to the core of my self-worth and my emotions bleed out. Yep, these kinds of situations can bring out the very worst in me. I can be wretched when someone messes with my family.

Our mama-bear reactions may come from a good place, but too often they come out sideways. And we tend to have long memories when it comes to others hurting those we love. We say mean things. We speak unkind words about others, gossiping to anyone who will listen. This misguided sense of protection can breed negativity and cynicism in the best of us. And even worse, it's misusing authenticity in the name of honesty.

Here's the problem with this course of action. Negative Nelly isn't who God created us to be, and choosing to see the glass half empty doesn't allow us to shine our true selves. It goes against the way our Creator wants us to live.

We know hard times are inevitable, but a negative attitude doesn't have to be.

You and I were designed with a complex set of emotions, but sometimes we overuse or misuse them, and we sin. Even more, negativity from that one situation can hemorrhage into every other situation or relationship we encounter. Negativity tends to bleed into. . .everywhere.

Now take a deep breath as I challenge you with this next question. Have you ever considered that God *allows* the tough seasons and situations in your life for a reason, that they have a divine purpose?

Luke 22:31 confirms that the Enemy must get permission before he can bring these hardships into our lives. Jesus is speaking to Peter when he says, "Peter, my dear friend, listen to what I'm about to tell you. Satan has demanded to come and sift you like wheat and test your faith" (TPT). That means every single heartache that comes your way—that comes my way—is preapproved by God. This isn't proof that God is mean; it's proof that God is so very good.

The truth is the Lord isn't as concerned with your comfort as much as He is concerned with your character. God is always in relentless pursuit of your heart and healing. And that sometimes means He allows hard things, knowing He can use them in powerful ways to accomplish His plans in you. But then we're required to find the grit and grace to trample the negatives and trust God's plan even when we can't fully understand it.

James encourages us with these words:

Don't run from tests and hardships, brothers and sisters. As difficult as they are, you will ultimately find joy in

them; if you embrace them, your faith will blossom under pressure *and teach you true patience as you endure.
And true patience brought on by endurance* will equip
you *to complete the long journey and cross the finish
line—mature, complete, and wanting nothing.*
(James 1:2–4 VOICE, emphasis mine)

I know, this asks a lot of us. Scriptures like this aren't for
the faint of heart. But you're made of good material and can
handle the truth. How do I know? Because you've read this
far into the book. That tells me you want truth, and so I'm
going to bring it. Ready?

This powerful statement from James gets up in our business. In this passage, he's asking us to do hard things. Not
only that, but he's reminding us that God made you and me
with a built-in ability to *do* those hard things. And then he
finishes by telling us the result if we persevere.

Let's break it down into three parts.

1.   We must stand in the mess.

James is encouraging us to face the tricky situations life
brings our way rather than trying to find a way out. While
it may feel unbearable, we have the gumption to dig deep
and find the grit and grace to stick with it. Persevering will
eventually produce joy.

2.   We must embrace the test.

James is asking us to be present in our mess. Rather than
run from it, we are to grab onto God and walk into it. And
if we choose to accept what God has allowed to come our
way—knowing it's for our benefit and His glory—then our
faith will mature.

3. We must remember endurance in the quest.

James then shares the *why*, encouraging us that God will give us all we need to get through the mess. And after standing in the mess and embracing the test, our faith will prove authentic as a result. Keep in mind the goal isn't avoiding pain—that's not realistic or beneficial—but instead allowing it to make us complete.

Sometimes just a tweak in our perspective can help tame negativity. Seeing our situation from a divine viewpoint can usher in peace, knowing God has us in His sights. Because when we face tough situations head-on, our response often reveals our faith. Will we complain and be negative, or will we choose to rely on God's help? Will we grumble and protest, or will we ask God for strength and wisdom? Will we find the grit and grace to be the joyful and hopeful women we were made to be, or will we not?

Will we trample the negatives or adopt them?

I know you have every good reason to be cynical. Every day we face situations full of the potential to sour us. We interact with people who are angry, full of bitterness and hate. We're around some who are quick to judge and others full of rage. People are finding bravery hiding behind a screen and using social media to make rude comments. And it sometimes feels like a crime to have an opinion, especially if it's different from theirs. Living offended isn't hard to do.

A few weeks ago I sat down to watch an NFL game on TV. I'm originally from Texas, so football is in my blood. This was the first Sunday after President Trump tweeted his opinion that fans should boycott teams if their players knelt rather than stood during the national anthem. He also suggested team owners fire any players who knelt, because he believed they were showing disrespect to our nation.

Now, I am not taking a side. Honestly, I see valid viewpoints from both camps on this issue. But what saddened me was the negativity this controversy generated—on all sides. The media was griping. The players were protesting. The White House signaled their disapproval. The fans took sides. And for some reason, everyone felt the need to speak their mind. For the love, can't we just watch grown men carry a pig-skinned ball down the field and eat our chips and salsa like adults?

And do you know what's lost in all this mess? The fact that we're supposed to be on the same team. We're supposed to be free to express our own opinion and let our neighbor do the same. It should be okay that we think and believe different things. Instead of screaming our opinions in anger, wouldn't it make more sense to be quicker to listen? Isn't it okay to disagree? I mean, we were created to think for ourselves, right? God did make us to live authentic, yes?

And even more, we're the *United* States. But these days, we're anything but united. Instead, we are the *Negative* States, and it's exhausting.

You see, we're not mindless robots. Our Father made us to think and feel and interact with honesty. He helps us find the grit and grace to navigate those kinds of interactions well. And it shows confidence when we're able to be real with our thoughts about issues. But maybe we're too concerned with being heard instead of taking the time to hear. Maybe we're focusing on the wrong thing.

Do you ever wonder if maybe we're giving up civility for negativity?

Hall of Faith

If you've never read Hebrews 11, stop right now and sit in that passage of scripture for a bit. It's known as the Hall of Faith because those listed are recognized for their powerful belief in God. They had trust on steroids. These men and women give us beautiful examples of what being faithful looks like. Was it easy for them? No. Did they have every right to throw temper tantrums, blame God, have pity parties, take it out on others, and give up? *Yes.*

But what I appreciate the most is that they had enduring faith in the Lord rather than sinking into negativity because of their circumstances.

Let's look a little deeper. Verse 13 in the New International Version of the Bible says this: "All these people were still living by faith when they died. They *did not* receive the things promised" (emphasis mine). Abraham, Isaac, Jacob, Joseph, Moses and many others—they obeyed God based on their calling and a promise, yet died before their blessing came to be. Yikes.

Throughout their stories, we get to see their humanness from time to time. We see they questioned God and the tasks He asked them to walk out. We know they struggled with confidence and fear and a million other insecurities we still face today. But these champions in the faith chose not to live in negativity even when they had every good reason to complain and whine. Instead, they kept their gaze on God, and their attitudes followed suit.

In verse 39, we're told it was their willingness to do the hard things rather than sink into the negatives that was worthy of applause. "These were all commended for their faith, yet none of them received what had been promised" (NIV).

Do you know why they are commended? It's because they kept an eternal perspective on their earthly situation. They were overcomers, not give-uppers. They were positive pillars, not Negative Nellies. They were faith carriers, not faith buriers. Shall I continue, or do you get the point? (I'm a word nerd. I know. Thanks for loving me anyway.)

In all seriousness, think about how easy it would have been to complain. Some of these Hall of Faith-ers faced stoning, prison, beheadings, and being sawed in two. For some, their journey was grueling till the very end. Yet they endured. Maybe they grumbled here and there, but their overall response to hardship was faith—*not negativity*.

They chose to stay positive in the midst of a hard journey.

DANIEL

If anyone had reason to be negative, it was Daniel. Being plucked from his homeland of Jerusalem, where he was a good, God-fearing Jewish boy, and imported into the pagan culture of Babylon was a surefire way to turn one's positive attitude into a destructive one. You can read all the details in his self-titled book in the Bible.

But Daniel knew who he was—and who God was. While he was liked by the king and found favor in his court, his faith remained strong, as did his attitude. Regardless of the foreign culture he lived in, his identity was rooted in his Creator. Rather than sink into a depression because of his new normal, he continued to trust God. Instead of bowing to an earthly king, he continued to kneel to the heavenly King. No matter the state of the society surrounding him, Daniel stayed true to himself. He was unafraid to be authentic.

When a law was passed that outlawed prayer to God—a decree aimed directly at Daniel—he knew the risks but chose to remain steadfast in his faith. In his opinion, he had no option but to be real. Three times a day, he went to his knees in prayer, giving thanks and praising God just like he had done for years. And when his enemies caught Daniel praying, it looked like the end for our hero. The punishment was time in the lions' den to face certain death.

Okay, this would have been just one of the items on my complaint list already a mile long. I would have already been cranky about my new culture and its misguided norms. I would have already been depressed knowing others were trying to set me up to fail. And now facing the prospect of being eaten alive would have sealed the deal. Negative Nelly would have burst onto the scene in rare form. I would have lost the grit and the grace to shine.

Now, the king loved Daniel, which made following through with this decree all the harder. Just like our main character, he was set up too. And at the first light of the morning after Daniel's night in the lions' den, King Darius rushed to see if he was still alive. When the king heard the voice from behind the stone, this happened:

> *The king could hardly contain his excitement and joy.*
> *He ordered that Daniel be taken up out of the lions' den.*
> *He was removed and examined carefully, but not even*
> *a scratch was found on him—all because he put his trust*
> *in His God.* (Daniel 6:23 VOICE)

Daniel had every good reason to be negative about all he was asked to endure, just like the rest of the Hall of Faith-ers.

He had every reason to gossip to the king about those who set him up for a fall. He could have become bitter. But he chose to remain in a posture of faith, trusting that God had allowed this for Daniel's benefit and God's own glory.

Even more, Daniel's authenticity affected this pagan king in a profound way. His character stood out. And because the king realized God had closed the mouths of the lions to save Daniel's life, Darius did something amazing.

> *I decree that all people everywhere who live under my sovereign rule ought to tremble before and fear the God of Daniel. For He is the living God, and He will endure forever. His kingdom will never be overthrown; His reign will know no end. He saves and rescues those who fear Him, performing signs and wonders in heaven and on earth; for He has rescued His servant Daniel from the power of the lions.* (Daniel 6:26–27 VOICE)

Daniel had a winning attitude, and God honored it!

STEPHEN

I'm so in awe of this great man. His story is one of my favorites because he showed humility and resolve and epic trust in God. This is the perfect story to revisit when life gets crazy and you feel put out by someone.

When I first got into ministry, I thought God would protect me from harm—like I was some special prophet who deserved exceptional care. Ah, to be young and prideful. And stupid. Saying yes to God doesn't earn you special treatment at all.

No matter how you slice it, following after God is hard. It's takes grit and grace, and it's a choice we must make every day. Our steadfast faith is what keeps us from falling into the pit of despair when times get crunchy. Because regardless of what we're facing here and now, we know in the end we'll be in the presence of Jesus—forever.

Stephen knew that. Our hero—a man "full of faith and full of the Holy Spirit" according to Acts 6:5 (VOICE)—was chosen by a committee to take care of the needy by distributing food. And while he fulfilled that role with integrity, he also began preaching the Gospel with authority.

Verses 8–9 tell us, "Stephen continually overflowed with extraordinary grace and power, and he was able to perform a number of miraculous signs and wonders in public view. But eventually a group arose to oppose Stephen and the message to which his signs and wonders pointed" (VOICE). Yep, his obedience to God got him on the radar of the Synagogue of the Freedman (a group of Cyrenians, Alexandrians, and men from the provinces of Cilicia and Asia). They began to have debates over doctrine. And it didn't end well.

In Acts 6:10–11 (VOICE), we learn that "the Holy Spirit gave Stephen such wisdom in responding to their arguments that they were humiliated; in retaliation, they spread a vicious rumor: 'We heard Stephen speak blasphemies against Moses and God.'" They were publicly embarrassed and angered, so they began spreading rumors.

But Stephen didn't retaliate; he stayed true to himself. While his adversaries were giving in to negativity, he didn't. My guess is that he was so filled by God's Holy Spirit that there was no room left for pessimism. He was his most authentic when he was preaching the Good News. It was what he was created to do. And can't you just imagine all of heaven watching as Stephen proclaimed the Messiah to the masses? It gives me chill bumps.

Stirred up and offended, a group of people, including elders and scribes, dragged Stephen into the presence of the council, provided false testimony, and accused him of blasphemy.

Time out. If I had been able to keep perspective and patience up until now, this part of the story would have sent me over the edge. I would have probably been snarky with those who lied about me and cantankerous with the Sanhedrin for believing it. I may have even been irritable toward God for not taking care of me, especially since I was doing work *for Him.* Do you know what I mean?

But not Stephen. "The entire council turned its gaze on Stephen to see how he would respond. They were shocked to see his face radiant with peace—as if he were a heavenly messenger" (v. 15 VOICE). He just refused to let negativity get a foothold in his heart. He had every reason to be full of anger, but he was full of peace. I just love this. It challenges me.

Then Stephen began to recount the story of the Israelites and their leaders of the past (Abraham, Moses) and called out his haters for being nothing like these truly God-fearing Jews. The crowd eventually became furious.

I don't want to paraphrase this next part because it deeply inspires me to keep my eyes on God and not my circumstances. If you will, please breathe in this part of the story. And notice that even with all the anger from others, Stephen was unafraid to be himself. He was a Jesus-loving, God-fearing, Holy Spirit–embracing man. And I admire the beautiful example he offers of being authentic—regardless of circumstances.

But Stephen was filled with the Holy Spirit. Gazing

upward into heaven, he saw something they couldn't see:
the glory of God, and Jesus standing at His right hand.

Stephen: Look, I see the heavens opening! I see the
Son of Man standing at the right hand of God!

At this, they covered their ears and started shouting.
The whole crowd rushed at Stephen, converged on him,
dragged him out of the city, and stoned him. They laid
their coats at the feet of a young man named Saul, while
they were pelting Stephen with rocks.

Stephen (as rocks fell upon him): Lord Jesus, receive
my spirit.

Then he knelt in prayer, shouting at the top of his
lungs

Stephen: Lord, do not hold this evil against them!

Those were his final words; then he fell asleep in
death. (Acts 7:55–60 VOICE)

Even as the rocks were cracking his bones and beating
against his head, even as blood was pooling beneath him, he
kept an eternal perspective. Stephen prayed. He refused to
become negative, and he responded the way he was created
to respond.

Mind blown. Mic dropped.

JOSEPH

I just have to share one last Bible character with you. This
guy had a long life full of opportunities to give in to negativity.
Talk about enduring faith to the max. Let's jump in.

Joseph was the favorite son of Jacob, which set him up
to be hated by his own older brothers. To show how special he was to his father, Joseph received a special robe—"a

spectacularly colorful robe with long sleeves in it" (Genesis 37:3 VOICE). And when his brothers saw the blatant acts of favoritism, they "grew to hate him and couldn't find it in themselves to speak to him without resentment or argument" (v. 4 VOICE). That's a lotta hate.

Scripture also tells us the tension continued to fester and grow, and it eventually reached a boiling point. But rather than kill off Joseph, his siblings trapped him and sold him into Egyptian slavery. Then they concocted a lie to cover their tracks. All the in-between details can be found in Genesis 37–50.

Once in Egypt, Joseph was purchased by Potiphar, an officer of Pharaoh. Joseph earned his trust, became the favored slave, and was put in charge of everything Potiphar owned. But with his good looks, Joseph eventually caught the eye of his master's wife, who tried to seduce the slave. He refused. And in anger, she pointed to Joseph as the one trying to put the moves on her. Even though that lie landed him in prison, Joseph didn't become negative.

Once there, he found favor with the chief jailer, who placed him in charge of all the prisoners. Joseph was trusted, just like in Potiphar's house. And because he was able to interpret dreams, that skill set eventually landed him in front of Pharaoh. Joseph was brought to the palace to decipher a disturbing dream for the most powerful man in the land.

Pharaoh liked what he heard. And Genesis 41:40–41 tells us just how happy he was: "Therefore you will be in charge of my household. All of my people will report to you and do as you say. Only I, because I sit on the throne, will be greater than you. I hereby appoint you head over all of the land of Egypt" (VOICE). Within one day, Joseph went from prison to palace. He was thirty years old.

While he had every right to be, never once does the Word mention Joseph being negative. Even through all he endured, he held on to a positive perspective. I can imagine he had moments when anger or cynicism snuck in, but God didn't want to focus on that part of his story. He wanted for us to see that Joseph chose to find the grit and grace to stand in faith and shine.

There's no doubt he stood out. In every circumstance recorded in the Bible, Joseph stayed true to who he was. He held on to morals. He held on to honesty. And he didn't compromise his authentic self to fit in or make friends. From saying no to adultery to telling the hard truth with dream interpretation to forgiving his brothers, he refused to let bitterness engulf him.

But, *this* is the main point I want to share with you through Joseph's story. Even when hated by his brothers. . . even when sold into slavery. . .even when falsely accused. . . even when landing in prison. . .he was on track to being placed in a position that would save many lives. Of course he had no idea of God's grand plan, but had he given in to negativity, his story might have had a different outcome.

Your takeaway is this. When you find yourself in difficult situations and tough circumstances—just like we all do almost every day—watch your attitude. God may have every intention of using you in a mighty way, but clinging to anger or bitterness will almost always interfere. Negativity has a way of derailing us from God's plan. Find the grit and grace to discover the silver lining and trust His plan.

Even more, friend, negativity doesn't look good on you—or me. Matthew 5:14–15 tells us we are the light of the world. When we choose to shine in authentic ways, others will see God because of our actions. I didn't hear an amen, so let me repeat that in bold letters: **Your *authenticity* helps others see God.**

And a negative attitude isn't part of the DNA God supernaturally deposited in you. Nowhere in the Bible does it list being *snarky* as a spiritual gift. Crankiness is not a fruit of the Spirit. Seeing the glass half empty isn't one of the Ten Commandments.

Can you think of any other time our nation has needed a huge dose of positivity added into the mix? Sometimes it feels like we're on the brink of exploding. Everyone's fists are clenched. Voices are loud. Words are harsh. Our patience is wearing thin. But maybe—just maybe—if we choose to be the kind of women God created us to be, we can show others a better way to live.

> *If it is within your power, make peace with all people.*
> *Again, my loved ones, do not seek revenge; instead, allow*
> *God's wrath to make sure justice is served. Turn it over*
> *to Him. For the Scriptures say, "Revenge is Mine. I will*
> *settle all scores."...Never let evil get the best of you; instead,*
> *overpower evil with good.* (Romans 12:18–19, 21 VOICE)

I talked about these verses earlier in the book, but it bears repeating. This is a battle cry for us to be agents of change—change for the good. Everywhere we look, we see negative influences. And if we aren't standing firm in who we are, we're missing an opportunity to shine positivity into some dark places.

What are some ways we can be ourselves and bring encouragement to others? Let's look at a few:

1. Zip it up.

For some reason, many of us have decided it's important to insert our thoughts into every conversation. We think our voices and opinions must be shared, often without any filters. And honestly, social media has given us the perfect forum to be bold in our negativity.

We feel safe behind screens, don't we? And we're being bullies, reckless and hurtful with our words. Too often we're forgetting that real people with real feelings are on the other side.

More times than I care to count, hurtful comments have come my way. People have said the rudest things about a post on Facebook or on my blog. And while others might tell us to develop thicker skin, tangling words tangle self-worth no matter how we try to brush them off. Chances are you've had the same virtual hate come your way.

Think about your Facebook feed just this past week. I bet you've seen negative comments about someone's shopping trip, their children's school, a social or race issue, something the president did or didn't do, and a million other displays of displeasure. Please have an opinion, but it's not necessary to spread negativity all over the internet.

God just can't be pleased when we whine and complain all the time. He most certainly is not pleased when we aren't kind to one another. And when we air our grievances for the world to see, we're not glorifying Him.

Consider this from Colossians 4:6 in *The Message*: "Be gracious in your speech. The goal is to bring out the best in others in a conversation, not put them down, not cut them out." God didn't create us to be negative toward others. We can tell the truth without being mean-spirited about it. We can be honest without condemnation. We can open up about our feelings without sliming someone with our words.

Ask God for the grit and grace to know when to speak the truth laced with love and when to keep comments to yourself. Remember, we are agents of peace. That's who we were made to be.

2. Tone it down.

It's not mandatory to take a side on every issue. Gone are the days when we could share our opinion without bracing for battle. Almost without fail, someone with a differing opinion will speak up in ways that don't glorify God.

A few years ago, someone I knew very well called me out about a benign video I posted on Facebook. It wasn't even on my wall. It was a funny video I shared on my husband's wall. This person watched it and then sent me a scathing email about how offended they were by its contents.

I'm so careful about what I share publicly. For obvious reasons, I try to stay as neutral as possible. And this video fit into that category. Even more, I shared this with my husband, not her. That means she had to go directly to his Facebook wall to see it.

You can imagine my surprise when her email landed in my inbox. I was caught off guard by her anger and rudeness. Even if it was something she didn't like, was there really a reason to send me her thoughts—thoughts I never asked for? This wasn't the first time she had spoken out of turn, and it forever changed our relationship.

Listen, we don't have to be right all the time. While black-and-white issues exist, some gray ones also exist. Let's not spend our time pointing fingers at the side we believe is ethically, socially, or politically wrong. Let's not feel lofty in our position of moral authority, thinking we're better. And we may be on the right side of an issue, but it's our negativity toward others that can make it all wrong. Even more, that negativity can be sinful. That's not how God wants us to live.

Ephesians 4:26–27 reads, "When you are angry, don't let it carry you into sin. Don't let the sun set with anger in your heart or give the devil room to work" (voice). Maybe it would be good to tone down our gotta-be-right tendencies and work on loving others better.

The world needs authentic women who will find the grit and grace to shine. It needs women who will take responsibility for their own choices and decisions—women who will trample the negatives in their own lives. What a beautiful call to be real.

3.   Give it over.

The best thing we can do when we feel negativity begin to rise in us is to give it to God. Throughout His Word we're told He hears us when we cry out. And because of that, He is always available to you and me.

You see, when we let things like anger, envy, pride, unforgiveness, and hate infiltrate our minds, they become a driving force for our feelings. We ruminate, replaying them over and over and over again. Those feelings take root and begin to affect our choices. Friend, negativity deeply affects how we live our one and only life. And because we're here to shine for Jesus, we simply cannot be a witness for Him when our hearts are full of offense.

But here's truth. Changing from a negative attitude to a positive one takes time and perseverance. It doesn't happen overnight. For some, it's a lifelong struggle to keep their minds on the right track. And without God's intervention, it's almost impossible to have any kind of lasting change. We may have fits and starts and every good intention, but with God's help we can do this. He wants us to protect our thoughts.

> *Finally, brothers and sisters, fill your minds with beauty and truth. Meditate on whatever is honorable, whatever is right, whatever is pure, whatever is lovely, whatever is good, whatever is virtuous and praiseworthy.* (Philippians 4:8 VOICE)

Only God can renew our minds. We can ask Him to replace the negative thoughts with positive ones. We can ask Him for the courage to find and focus on the good. And we can ask for the grit to stand for peace and the grace to stand for truth.

It's important to remember that God doesn't often take sides on what we're getting bent out of shape about. He loves both the Dems and the GOP. He loves all races and both genders of people. He believes all lives matter. And He doesn't care if you kneel or stand during the national anthem.

So when we begin to feel our blood boil and our attitude taking a southern turn, let's ask God for peace to deal with the issues begging for our two cents every day. Let's ask for the wisdom to know when to engage and when to let go. And let's ask for the desire to be kind when we'd rather be right.

4. Love it out.

As I left to speak at a retreat earlier this year, I was in a cranky space. And while I love to stand on a stage and share what God is doing in my life, I wanted to hide under my covers at home instead.

Looking back, I realize how much God knew exactly what He was doing. From the moment I was picked up at the airport to the moment I was dropped off days later, these women loved on me. I was showered with pumpkin-spice snacks (my favorite). I was upgraded to a suite at the hotel. I was encouraged through words and gifts. I received hugs and smiles and fist bumps. Without even knowing how much I needed it, they showered me with love.

I walked into that retreat heavy and emotionally burdened, but their love freed me up to bring my authentic self to those women. It gave me courage to be my messy self from the stage. Their appreciation and support gave me grit and grace to find the confidence to shine Him into that room through my words and testimony. And that weekend helped me trample the negatives weighing me down. God used the love from a room full of strangers to help me find hope.

Something about blessing others makes us feel more positive about life. I sure hope they felt His delight as they loved me up. And while I may never know for sure, I think they did. That's just how God works. But whether we're on the receiving end of tenderness or the one passing it on, love can't help but cast aside negativity.

Listen, sweet one, the world has enough negatives. We already have enough reasons to live in defeat and discouragement. Negativity is running rampant in our hearts and homes. What if we chose to live authentically by revealing the positive nature of God through our own words and actions? What if we decided to bring hope to the hopeless and joy to the joyless by choosing our battles and by speaking kindly rather than angrily?

I'm not suggesting we present a counterfeit life when we're in the weeds. Nor do we have to share every difficulty to every person. But God made us to take Jesus into the world, and His message is a good one. Let's be careful not to dwell on the negative when we have so much to be positive about. We may have to dig deep to discover it, but we can always find something to be thankful for. Let's be women who find the gold in the middle of our mess.

FINDING THE GRIT

Would you say you're more negative or positive about your life and the world around you?

In what ways does being negative help your situation? How does it hurt it?

We looked at the James 1:2–4 passage in detail. What stood out to you the most and why?

How can a shift in your perspective change the way you see your circumstance?

What Bible character's story spoke to you through this chapter?

How does trampling the negatives help you live authentic?

FINDING THE GRACE

Father, we have so many reasons to be negative. I sometimes feel overwhelmed by the weight of the world or my own life. Forgive me for being discouraged and not asking for Your help. I know You care about what my heart cares about. I want to bring hope and joy into the hard circumstances others are facing. I want to shine Your light into trials and tribulations, helping others see where You are in their mess. Even more, I need to remember to look for the silver lining, because if I look deep enough, I'll find one. Help me be positive and trample the negatives that try to infiltrate my heart and mind. In Jesus' mighty name I pray, amen.

Live
Accept Your Awesomeness
Unearth the Untruths
Try Loving Everyone
Hold on to Hope
Embrace and Extend Forgiveness
Never Shrink Back
Trample the Negatives
I
C

CHAPTER 11

Invest in Community

Alone we can do so little; together we can do so much.
—Helen Keller [14]

I recently went to a women's conference with high hopes of refueling my passion for doing what God had set before me. It was designed specifically for ministry-minded women who write and speak, geared toward nourishing and equipping us. Honestly, don't we *all* need that?

As women, we so often pour out every bit of patience and encouragement and wisdom we have—and it leaves us feeling like a pile of dry bones. Whether your ministry is standing on stages, writing books, leading small groups, managing family schedules, or standing in the gap for a friend, we are each called to serve the Kingdom with our one and only life. And sometimes we get weary.

In the few weeks leading up to the retreat, I was feeling expectant for God to meet me in that room full of women. I was sure I'd make some divine connections, creating unexpected friendships. I was looking forward to stepping out of the daily grind for a few days and resting in the Lord while encouraged by new community.

Yeah, it didn't quite happen that way.

Community looks different for everyone. If you're an extrovert, chances are you thrive in the chaos of people being all around. You love the flurry of conversations and laughter, soaking in every interaction that comes your way. The more people you meet, the better. The more necks you hug, the sweeter. The more connections you make, the happier. Gosh, I admire your ability to jump in with both feet.

But maybe you're more of the introverted persuasion. You are the one—*I am the one*—who enjoys a good friend in a corner of the room. Others will always find us on the outside of the big groups, trying to look like we're not completely freaked out by the mass of people as far as the eye can see. We're the ones who blossom when we're all alone. The introverted love to connect to community with purpose and intentionality, and then retreat as soon as possible. (Don't interpret our need for solace as an indication that we don't love community. We do. Just in smaller doses.)

Some are a sweet mix of both. According to Merriam-Webster, your official title is an ambivert. You're the hybrids. You're the functioning introvert or the contemplative extrovert. You can rise to the occasion and rock it every time. Oh, I like you.

Regardless, God made each of us with a certain temperament. It's our authentic person. It's how our Creator wanted us to interact with the world. Being an introvert or a hybrid doesn't give us permission to opt out of community. It just means our people-ing looks a little different from an extrovert's. One is not the right way or the wrong way. It just *is*. And I bet if you really dug into your life experiences and your gifting, you'd see how the specific temperament God gave you perfectly equips you. It's pretty cool.

Well, I walked into that conference with big hopes and extrovert expectations, but it was oddly uncomfortable right from the start. There were a lot of smiling women ready to hug my neck and shake my hand. They were all up in my personal space as they tried to introduce themselves over the roar of voices in the room. I was overwhelmed with new names and unfamiliar faces. And while I knew they loved Jesus and had every good intention of creating an environment to usher in His presence, I also knew it just wasn't my jam.

I realized quickly this wasn't what would fill me up. As much as I wanted to, I just couldn't muster the grit and grace to push through, knowing this wasn't going to breathe life into my dry bones. This wasn't a situation where I would shine authenticity. I wouldn't be able to be myself in this sea of women.

Oh, but God was up to something beautiful. Sweet mercy, He always has my back. And what happened instead was so unexpected. I realized on the back end of the weekend that He used my conference hopes to get me there so He could restore me with the most unforeseen gift of community.

I'm learning that community comes in all sorts of shapes and sizes. Sometimes we need big community, and other times we relish in the few women God brings our way. It can be simple or complex. We can have casual friendships or steady Eddies. Community can be all about fun, or we can dig into the seriousness of life, wading into deeper waters.

It can be full of truth-tellers who hold us accountable or friends who just want to escape life at a coffee date. It can be our workmates, our neighbors, or our yoga class. Community can happen as we sit for chemotherapy, gather for a common cause, or wait in line for concert tickets. Yes, we can connect for a million different reasons. And that connecting can have an impact on our lives for the better.

I'll be honest. I skipped most of the conference and hung out with a few women I'd met online through ministry groups. We may have been from different parts of the country, but we had a common goal to share the love of Jesus with the world. Over the previous several months, we'd been praying together, revealing bits and pieces of our struggles, encouraging one another with scripture, and sharing everyone's work with our own audiences. It was such a blessing to find like-minded community to partner with.

Matthew 18:19–20 says, "When two of you get together on anything at all on earth and make a prayer of it, my Father in heaven goes into action. And when two or three of you are together because of me, you can be sure that I'll be there" (MSG). Even God knows the value and power of community.

Over those few days, we laughed until we almost peed our pants, ate Mexican food until we almost barfed, and shared our burdens until we cried. We stayed up late talking and slept in past breakfast. And a few of us even got tattoos. I came home full.

Yes, friend, sometimes community feels like a great investment. And times like these make connecting easy and exciting. Think about it. It's easy to love when people are lovable. It's easy to be together when no one rocks the boat.

But what happens when community has wounded you? How do you muster the grit and grace to be yourself when you feel offended, unseen, unheard, or misunderstood?

WHY DO WE NEED TO EMBRACE COMMUNITY WHEN IT'S DIFFICULT?

The easy thing to do is to walk away. Gosh, I've done that way too many times. But there's something to be said about having a stick-to-it mentality. It allows us to build real community together. We need to decide there really is value in being there for one another, even when it requires more of us than we'd like to offer up. It takes genuine love to step into the crunchiness of another's situation when walking away can often feel so much better.

Authentic love is messy because it's real and raw and honest. And authentic women choose to love authentically. First John 4:7–12 tells us why.

> *My loved ones, let us devote ourselves to loving one another. Love comes straight from God, and everyone who loves is born of God and truly knows God. Anyone who does not love does not know God, because God is love.*
>
> *Because of this, the love of God is a reality among us: God sent His only Son into the world so that we could find true life through Him. This is the embodiment of true love: not that we have loved God first, but that He loved us and sent His unique Son on a special mission to become an atoning sacrifice for our sins.* So, my loved ones, if God loved us so sacrificially, surely we should love one another. *No one has ever seen God with human eyes; but if we love one another, God truly lives in us.*

Consequently God's love has accomplished its mission among us. (VOICE, emphasis mine)

In this passage, John reminds us that loving others requires commitment. I'm not sure any of us would argue with that. Amen? He then digs into this idea of love and why we can offer it to others. In a nutshell, John tells us God is love, we can love only because of Him, loving others proves we are His, and Jesus bridged the gap sin created so we could stay in God's love. Then he brings home the gold, telling us why we need to love community even when it's difficult.

Sink your teeth into this: since God loved us sacrificially (Christ's death on the cross), we need to honor Him by loving others—even the hard-to-love others. *This is where our grit and grace come into play.* And John goes on to say that when we do, it makes our ability to love stronger. *This is where we shine.*

We love community—invest in community—because it shows great consideration for God and His prized creation. When God made you and me, He baked in the ability to love those around us, which encourages authentic fellowship with others. And even more, love has God's supernatural power to change us, bless us, heal us, and connect us to His heart. Yes, community is good for us! It's beneficial for you and me.

Need proof? Let's unpack five compelling reasons investing our time and energy in community matters.

1. Community supports our emotional needs.

Think of those times you just needed someone to listen to your heart. Or times you needed a friend to help you work through an issue. Or when you needed someone safe to cry with— somebody you could open up to about hard circumstances.

If we let it, community can be a place where we're free to reveal our true selves, and it's a gift from God. It can encourage us to let down our guard and be unafraid to be ourselves. Galatians 6:2 tells us, "Share each other's troubles and problems, *and so obey our Lord's command*" (TLB, emphasis mine).

2. Community teaches us how to navigate conflicts.

When we look at the state of the world, it seems obvious we're not doing a good job of navigating conflict. Everyone is offended. And instead of listening, so many of us are shouting our opinions and ideas at each other. But this isn't how God wants it to be. His plan is for us to work through life together in positive ways.

First Corinthians 1:10 says, "My brothers and sisters, I urge you by the name of our Lord Jesus, the Anointed, to *come together* in agreement. Do not allow anything or anyone to create division among you. Instead, be restored, completely *fastened together with one mind* and *shared judgment*" (VOICE, emphasis mine).

We can choose to connect with honesty and respect, sharing our true hearts with one another. Yes, we really can be real with others. Done right, community can be a sweet reminder that we are on the same team, and that those with different ideas and opinions aren't necessarily the enemy.

3. Community grows our forgiveness muscle.

If there is one thing community does for us, it's provide ample opportunities to forgive. Do I hear an amen in the house today? Not only do we need to extend grace, but we need it too.

Listen to this: "Make a clean break with all cutting, backbiting, profane talk. Be gentle with one another, sensitive. *Forgive one another* as quickly and thoroughly as God in Christ forgave you" (Ephesians 4:32 MSG, emphasis mine).

Community calls us to a higher standard of living and loving. It can be the source of our most painful memories as well as the catalyst for our very best ones. And because we're so often encouraged to be authentic with our tribe, getting hurt is inevitable. Don't let that be a deterrent. We can always muster the grit and grace to choose forgiveness, and community will be the first to help us grow that muscle.

4. Community helps us be more like Christ.

Community refines us by challenging us. Being in a relationship with others can be difficult because it constantly requires give and take on both sides. Proverbs 27:17 says, "In the same way that iron sharpens iron, a person sharpens the character of his friend" (VOICE). God uses this supernatural process to help us become the women He designed us to be. Yet sometimes we just don't want any more character. Amen?

But the Lord never leaves us where we are. He—in all His wisdom—employs those we love to help transform our rough edges. He lets conflict within community teach us how to love better. He even uses it to heal some of our greatest wounds. And because God loves us so, He uses community to refine our character to reflect more of Jesus.

5. Community takes our eyes off ourselves.

If we're in community with others, we can't help but see the needs of those around us. From giving a hug to offering a prayer to delivering a meal to helping with bills, being part of a fellowship of people gives us a new perspective on life. It opens our eyes and our hearts to those who need help.

Proverbs 22:9 says, "Generous people are genuinely blessed because they share their food with the poor" (voice). What a great reminder that choosing to be selfless brings the delight of the Lord. Community is a powerful tool He uses to bring help and relief to those who need it the most. And it touches deep places in our hearts when we invest in community altruistically, because selflessness is part of our authentic person—the person God made us to be.

As I read the Bible, it is glaringly apparent that God's people have a hard time loving one another and doing life together well. Think about it:

- Cain murdered his brother Abel.
- Noah's community laughed at and mocked him.
- The Israelites were always whining about something.
- Job's wife didn't stand by her man.
- Joseph had a love/hate relationship with his siblings.
- King Saul and David rarely saw eye to eye.
- Jesus' disciples argued about various things.
- The New Testament churches fought regularly.

But on the flip side, some characters in the Bible—faith-filled men and women who loved others well and poured their hearts and souls into their well-being—truly valued community. One man, however, stands out the most.

And what stirs me is that while he wasn't even in the same country as his beloved community, his heart was so very much for them. He longed for his people to honor God's commands because he knew it was vital. His name is Ezra.

We'll probably need a little backstory, so let me set the stage.

Do you remember the story of King Nebuchadnezzar? While he's mentioned and referenced throughout the Bible, you can find his story in the first four chapters of Daniel. And both our history books and God's Word agree that powerful Nebuchadnezzar was anything but kind. He was known as ruthless.

This king was credited with the destruction of Judah and Jerusalem in 586 BC. He destroyed the temple, demolished the city wall, and took the privileged class back to Babylon. These Jewish, God-fearing men and women were thrown into a pagan culture. And it went against everything they knew.

Eventually, Nebuchadnezzar and the Babylon Empire were overthrown by Cyrus and the Medo-Persian Empire. And with the new regime came a surprising decree. After seventy years of captivity, the exiled Jews were now free. They could leave Babylon and return to their beloved home-land of Jerusalem.

Zerubbabel was tasked by God to lead the first wave of Israelites—about fifty thousand of the two million Jews in Babylon—back home. They were to rebuild the temple and restore worship in the city. And while they had a few bumps and bruises along the way, they completed what they set out to do.

But even though the temple had been rebuilt and worship

reinstated, life in Jerusalem was still a mess. Their building project hadn't fixed the problems within the community itself. They were living in defiance of God's laws—the ones He was *very* clear about. And Ezra knew it. His heart ached to bring the community of Israelites living in Jerusalem into alignment with God's will. He was deeply invested in them.

While Ezra was a Levite and his ancestry traced back to Aaron (Moses' brother), he was a scribe in Babylon. This meant he was well versed in the Law of Moses and knew what God expected and wanted from His people. His heart was burdened for the spiritual growth and integrity of his community. And this concern began to consume his thoughts until he finally asked the king for permission to travel to Jerusalem.

Once the trip was approved, he gathered an additional eight thousand Jews to return home with him. Ezra was ready to restore a community that had drifted far from God.

And drifted they had! The worst-case scenario was true and real. Ezra 9:2 says, "The Israelites, priests, Levites, and even our chiefs have intermarried with the daughters of non-Jews" (VOICE). Even more, they adopted their pagan culture.

Now, Ezra knew God had forbidden intermarriage for the Israelites (Exodus 34:15–16). Moses warned them again before they entered Canaan. They knew it was wrong, but they didn't care. It wasn't a case of racial prejudice but one of spiritual purity. Do you know why? Because this was the lineage to which Jesus Christ would come into the world.

When Ezra discovered this mess, it knocked him to his knees. He was heartbroken for his community. According to Ezra 9:3, he tore his tunic and cloak and pulled hair from his head and beard. And he sat in "stunned silence" all day. Ezra knew how gracious and faithful God had always been to them, and they returned His love with deliberate disobedience.

Let's take a break here. This revelation really messed up Ezra, didn't it? And it makes me wonder if maybe you can relate. Can you think of a time someone you deeply loved and cared for—someone you invested time and energy in—made choices that absolutely broke your heart?

Maybe you were betrayed in marriage or your child turned his back on the faith you raised him with.

Maybe your friend started drinking again or your sister disconnected from the family.

Maybe your tribe left you off the party invite or someone shared your secret.

Maybe someone promised to handle something one way but didn't, and now you feel betrayed.

Hands down, the hardest part about a community investment is being let down. And when you let your heart fill with hopes and dreams for how it could be, you're often let down by how it actually is. Friend, it takes grit and grace to love a community that has let you down. It may not be our natural response, but God baked the ability into us. That means we can access that kind of love with God's help.

If you'd been Ezra, the one to discover the truth and suffer the heartache from it, what would you have done? After sitting in silence like he did, what would you have done next? Would you have lashed out, verbally berating everyone? Would you have shamed and guilted them for their stupid choices? Would you have given up, turned around, and gone back to life as you knew it?

You know what Ezra did? He prayed.

Sometimes the most powerful investment we can make in our community is to pray for it. When we tap into our true concerns and lay them before God—be they for the world, our nation, our states, our cities, our neighborhoods, our churches, or our families—He listens. And taking the time to pray reveals our authentic hearts for those we care about. It's an opportunity to be real with God about things that matter most to our hearts. And it helps shine heaven down on people and situations that need His attention.

Scripture tells us that when Ezra discovered the outright sin of his community, he fell to his knees with his hands spread out to the Lord, and he prayed. This wasn't a normal, everyday prayer. No, it was the knee-callousing kind of prayer. This prayer was of the white-knuckle variety. He was in tears as he bowed on the steps of the temple. And others joined him, weeping as he cried out to God.

I know this prayer is a big block of copy and begging you to skip over it, but please don't. It's power-packed with authenticity. And I want to encourage you to underline or highlight the parts of Ezra's plea that speak to your heart the most. Soak in the prayer he prayed for his community that day.

O my True God, witness my shame and embarrassment as I appeal to You. My True God, our sins are so great that they have flooded over us, and they have reached to the heavens. Our people are chronic sinners, our sin is greater than we could have imagined, and You have tried to correct our behavior by subjecting our kings and our priests to death, captivity, theft, and shame by foreign rulers. Those pagans continue to rule us today. Even though You, our Eternal God, have shown Your grace by preserving a remnant and by giving us a secure hold in Your holy place, may You, our God, brighten our eyes and grant us assurance even in our bondage to the Persian rulers. We are still their slaves. In this bondage, You, our True God, have not forgotten us; Your loyal love inspired the kings of Persia to allow us to rebuild Your house and the walls to provide protection in Judah and Jerusalem.

But in spite of Your love, we have abandoned Your commands, and we have no excuse. You warned us through Your servants, the prophets, that the land of Canaan was polluted with pagans, that their evil actions had removed anything pure or good there, even filling up the land from end to end with horrible practices. You warned us not to marry our children to theirs, to seek treaties with them, or to covet their prosperity so that we would remain strong as a nation and as individuals, eating good foods from the earth and leaving that earth to Your children always.

In spite of Your mercy toward us—You, our True God, did not punish us as much as our obvious guilt and our evil actions required and have freed these exiles— once again we have ignored Your commands. We married pagans and have taken on their horrible practices, knowing that Your anger would motivate You to destroy every last Jew without leaving any remnant people.

Eternal God of Israel, You are righteous and justified in everything You do. Today we are nothing but the preserved remnant who escaped Your wrath, and today we confess our guilt. None of us should be able to stand and be acquitted before You. (Ezra 9:6–15 VOICE)

I love the realness of this prayer. It's raw and honest. It's so authentic. And I hope you read it out loud, because sometimes it helps to hear these kinds of words spoken aloud. If you didn't, please consider rereading it with full voice, remembering how broken Ezra was when he cried these words to God that day.

You know, Ezra said all the things the Israelites should have said to their heavenly Father. He spoke truth and confessed everything before the Lord. He laid it all out there on behalf of his countrymen. Oh, how he loved his community. And something he did during this prayer really connected to my heart.

Did you notice that he lumped himself into the wrongdoing? Where I may have used the word *them*, Ezra used the words *we* and *us*. I love that about him. This reveals how invested he really was. He hadn't been the one to commit the crime, but he was committed to standing as one with his community.

His heart was so with them that he included himself as one of them.

Let's take a giant step back and ask an important question. How might our community prosper if we decided to work together instead of blaming everyone else for a mess we find ourselves in? What if we saw each other as teammates? What if we rallied around one another when a moral failure happens rather than point fingers and criticize? It would be exactly like God planned it to be.

Not only did Ezra's prayer rock heaven, but it rocked the heart of the community too. While they'd recognized and confessed their sins, they couldn't escape the consequences of them. And you won't believe what they decided to do.

"We shall make a new covenant with our True God, promising to banish our foreign wives and their children" (Ezra 10:3 VOICE). And they did.

Had Ezra not been so burdened for his community, the lawlessness may have continued and forever tainted the lineage Jesus was to come from. His investment of care and concern brought about reconciliation for God's chosen people. One man is credited with the restoration of the Israelite community in Jerusalem, and that man is Ezra.

Friend, I know community is messy. It has the power to expose our insecurities and encourage counterfeit living. I understand how painful it can be, because most of my deepest wounds come from it. Yours probably do too. But God created community on purpose and for a purpose. And He uses it to bless us and shape us. He uses it to heal us and break us. It encourages us and challenges us. Community is a source of both joy and heartache.

Even more, community provides an opportunity to create the kind of authenticity that satisfies those deep places in our souls. It allows us to be seen and known. We get to wade into deep waters with like-minded women. It validates our existence and helps us be our real selves in a world that tells us to fit into a box. As women, that's one of our greatest needs. The only way community works is when we choose to invest in it.

Let's be unafraid to jump back into community. I promise it's worth the risk. And when we ask God for the grit and grace to love and trust again, He will provide it. Let's give community a break. Rather than set unrealistic expectations of perfection, let's release others from the burden of filling us in areas only God can. It's not fair or realistic. And it sets us up to be wounded, urging us to run in the other direction.

Friend, let's remember that we're all broken people living in a broken world trying to navigate broken relationships. Community isn't about perfection. It's about finding a place where we can reveal our authentic selves and be loved—stumbles, fumbles, and all.

And last, not only is it refreshing to find a place where we can be real, but it encourages others to do the same. True community tells us we don't have to live fake, looking like we have it all together. We can choose to live loud and proud as the amazing (and imperfect) women God made us to be.

FINDING THE GRIT

What are your thoughts on community? What does it look like in your life? What's missing?

Would you say you're extroverted, introverted, or ambiverted? How does community fit into that?

Community can be hard and wounding, and no one is exempt from the pain it can throw our way. What encouragement have you received to help you navigate difficult relationships?

We talked about five ways community benefits us. What did you learn? What surprised you the most?

What nuggets did you find in Ezra's prayer? How did his story speak to your thoughts on community?

How does investing in community help you live authentic?

FINDING THE GRACE

Father, thank You for making community. I know it was an intentional design that has great purpose in my life. And even though it's tricky at times, I need it. Would You heal me of the times it's wounded me in the past? Would You bring divine perspective when I need it the most? Would you rekindle the desire to open my heart to others, forgiving the times I've been hurt? I want to be the kind of woman who loves others well and who engages community in godly ways. I want to love rather than hold on to offenses that make me want to hide away from others. Thank You for including Ezra's story in the Bible. He shows us a beautiful example of being burdened for the hearts of others. I want to be like that for my friends and family. Help me find authentic community where I can be myself, and help me be someone who encourages others to be who You created them to be. In Jesus' mighty name I pray, amen.

Live
Accept Your Awesomeness
Unearth the Untruths
Try Loving Everyone
Hold on to Hope
Embrace and Extend Forgiveness
Never Shrink Back
Trample the Negatives
Invest in Community
C

CHAPTER 12

Camp in the Word of God

*A Bible that's falling apart usually
belongs to someone who isn't.*
—Charles H. Spurgeon[15]

Sam and Sara were born only fourteen months apart. And while the first year was hard with one child up during the night and the other awake most of the day, I really do love how close in age—and in friendship—these two are.

Sam would play Barbies with his younger sister, and Sara would build LEGO spaceships with her older brother. They were two peas in a pod—best friends. And she hung on his every word. If Sam said it, it was truth. Period.

One day I heard them talking from another room. Their sweet, high-pitched voices delighted my heart. And while they were kindergarten-aged at the time, their conversation sounded like two professionals in a serious meeting.

Sara: *Are you serious, Sam? I didn't know that.*

Sam: *Yes, it's true. We are made of chicken.*

Sara: *So we have chicken meat inside us? Not people meat?*

Sam: *Right. Chicken meat. We are made of chicken. That's just the way it is.*

Enter Mom.

Me: *Actually, we are not made of chicken. Chickens are made of chicken. We are people.*

Sara: *No, Mom. Sam said we're made of chicken. So we have chicken meat inside us.*

Me: *Sara, think about it. If we had chicken meat inside us, that would make us chickens. Are you a chicken? No. You are human. So that means we have people stuff inside us.*

Sam: *We're full of chicken meat, Mom. It's just the truth.*

Sara: *Yeah. I believe Sam.*

Exit Mom. Giggling.

I knew these two wouldn't leave for college believing that crazy logic, so I decided to let it go. It was obvious there was nothing I could do or say that would convince my kids otherwise. Sara was going to rely on Sam for her anatomy information rather than digging for the truth herself.

Sometimes we can be like that too. Sometimes we decide to blindly believe what others tell us God says in the Bible. We get our Word for the day from a devotional or book instead of opening the Bible for ourselves. We listen to podcasts or webinars and choose to take everything they say as God's truth. Rather than spending our own time in scripture, we get lazy and let others feed us. We absorb their interpretation as our truth. And while that may be a convenient way to live, it's also a scary way.

Here's a powerful truth I want you to know. You—*yes, even you*—have been given the ability to read and understand scripture. As Jesus-girls, the Holy Spirit in us brings the revelation and knowledge we need to make sense of scripture. While teachers may have insight and offer ways to apply godly ideas in our everyday lives, we don't need to rely solely on others for interpretation or understanding.

I know scripture can feel overwhelming at times because parts are written in ways you and I don't normally speak. Some of it is straight-up confusing. And even more, some scripture is scary and hard to reconcile in your heart and mind. I'm right there with you. I face the same struggles with parts of the Bible.

You know what I do when I'm grappling to understand a verse or passage? I read that same verse or passage in different translations or paraphrases, just as I often share them throughout this book. Of course, I have my favorites, but sometimes reading a passage translated differently helps me grasp its significance better. I'll even look up meaty words within a passage to make sure I know what they mean or find familiar synonyms. Friend, I'm encouraging you to do the same when you feel overwhelmed by any part of scripture.

Regardless of whether you're a scholar or a socialite (or someone in between), God created scripture to reveal Himself. This Book was written for us. This is where we learn about God's character. The Bible offers documented moments and seasons of His faithfulness. It unpacks His story. And God intended for it to be our guide—a divine blueprint, if you will—as we walk out this one and only life on planet Earth.

Second Timothy 3:16–17 backs this up. It reads, "All of Scripture is God-breathed; in its inspired voice, we hear useful teaching, rebuke, correction, instruction, and training for a life that is right so that God's people may be up to the task ahead and have all they need to accomplish every good work" (VOICE). Without a doubt, the Bible is a powerful tool for you and me.

Timothy is offering us a few good reminders:

- While God chose men to pen the scriptures, He is the author of every word, idea, thought, and command.
- All scripture has value and helps us in our everyday lives.
- God's Word gives us everything we need to do the task before us.

As I write this book, we're in a season of watching several well-known, well-loved pillars in the faith change course. Some have taken a nose-dive with their faith, facing public moral failures. Others have tweaked scripture ever so slightly to support their new narrative. And others have decided

God's Word is out-of-date, suggesting it's completely irrelevant in some places. Sweet mother of Abraham, it's such an interesting time to be alive.

Do you see the danger here? Unless we know what the Word of God says, we'll be the ones following these leaders right off the cliff of deception. We'll adopt their misguided teachings as truth and possibly pass it down to the next generation. And if we don't know what the Bible says, we won't know if what we're hearing is true. Even more, if we don't camp in scripture, we won't have pertinent passages written on our hearts and available at a moment's notice. At every turn, we need His words to penetrate our hearts and minds.

How does the Word of God help you?

It tells you who you are.

Within the pages of the Bible are powerful truths about who you are—and who you are not. This is where you find the truth of your authentic self. This is where you learn about how and why God created you. In these pages you discover your value and worth in the eyes of your Creator. This is where you find the courage to be who God created you to be—again, stumbles, fumbles, and all. This is where you'll learn your true identity. Here is a sampling:

> *I will offer You my grateful heart, for I am Your unique creation, filled with wonder and awe. You have approached even the smallest details with excellence; Your works are wonderful; I carry this knowledge deep within my soul.* (Psalm 139:14 VOICE)

> *Know this: the Eternal One Himself is the True God.*

He is the One who made us; we have not made ourselves;
we are His people, like sheep grazing in His fields.
(Psalm 100:3 VOICE)

It helps you take the next right step.

The Bible is just as relevant today as it was thousands of years ago, and it's chock-full of wisdom for every situation you will face. It's complete and infallible. I can't think of one struggle you may be facing that isn't addressed in its pages. Every relational situation or financial frustration or personal aggravation you deal with is addressed by scripture. And when you dig into the Word for help, you'll always find direction or inspiration or wisdom. Here are a few reminders:

> *Your word is a lamp for my steps; it lights the path before me.* (Psalm 119:105 VOICE)

> *If you don't have all the wisdom needed* for this journey, *then all you have to do is ask God for it; and God will grant all that you need. He gives lavishly and never scolds you for asking.* (James 1:5 VOICE)

> *Place your trust in the Eternal; rely on Him completely; never depend upon your own ideas and inventions.* (Proverbs 3:5 VOICE)

It becomes your moral compass.

God's Word reveals what is right and what is wrong. It reminds you that righteous indignation can quickly twist into sin. It points out selfishness and impure motives. It tells you what earthly traps to avoid. The Bible doesn't sugarcoat or make you read between the lines. It's very clear about the importance of keeping yourself right with God. Check these out:

Deep within me I have hidden Your word so that I will never sin against You. (Psalm 119:11 VOICE)

But don't be so naïve—there's another saying you know well—Bad company corrupts good habits.
(1 Corinthians 15:33 VOICE)

O how terrible for those who confuse good with evil, right with wrong, light with dark, sweet with bitter.
(Isaiah 5:20 VOICE)

It renews your mind.

It's so easy to let the world influence your thoughts. Gosh, we're bombarded with its messages every day. This constant barrage of negativity and offensiveness tangles us up, making us believe untruths about who we are. It confuses us about who God is. And it skews the truth about what is right and what is wrong. As a result, we get stuck in unhealthy thought patterns.

These patterns tell us we're not okay. They tell us to change who we are so we can be better. They encourage us to strive for acceptance and approval. And they can make us feel worthless.

But the Bible counters the lies. It tells you the truth. It reminds you of your value. It gives you courage to be yourself. It gives you courage to love who God made you to be. It gives you permission to be you. Here's what I mean:

*Do not allow this world to mold you in its own image.
Instead, be transformed from the inside out by renewing
your mind. As a result, you will be able to discern what
God wills and whatever God finds good, pleasing, and
complete.* (Romans 12:2 VOICE)

*And I will give you a new heart—I will give you new
and right desires—and put a new spirit within you. I
will take out your stony hearts of sin and give you new
hearts of love.* (Ezekiel 36:26 TLB)

It reveals God's character.

God is good, all the time. Even when you don't understand His will or agree with His ways, God is faithful. Even
when you can't see His divine hand in your situation, God
is trustworthy. Even when you can't comprehend why He
allows such evil to take place, God is sovereign. Yes, God
is good all the time, and when you read His Word, you're
reminded of that time and time again. You get to read His
story and see God's loyalty and devotion to His children.

And I don't know about you, but I need to be reminded
that He's got the whole world in His hands. I need to be
reminded that God is in control, that I am forgiven, and that
He loves me even in my imperfection. I need to know that
He made me on purpose, and that who I am is acceptable.
Check this out:

*The Eternal is compassionate and merciful. When
we cross all the lines, He is patient with us. When we
struggle against Him, He lovingly stays with us—
changing, convicting, prodding; He will not constantly*

criticize, nor will He hold a grudge forever. Thankfully, God does not punish us for our sins and depravity as we deserve. In His mercy, He tempers justice with peace. Measure how high heaven is above the earth; God's wide, loving, kind heart is greater for those who revere Him. You see, God takes all our crimes—our seemingly inexhaustible sins—and removes them. As far as east is from the west, He removes them from us. An earthly father expresses love for his children; it is no different with our heavenly Father; The Eternal shows His love for those who revere Him. (Psalm 103:8–13 VOICE)

There's never been a time I've closed my Bible and thought, *Well, that was a waste of my time.* I have never felt hopeless after reading scripture. I've never sat in the Word and felt defeated, as though I should give up and move on. Every time I have camped in the Bible, I've been encouraged and affirmed. I've found strength and wisdom. I've felt peace and comfort. And it's that closeness to my Creator that breeds authentic living, because I find the confidence and courage to be *me*.

I'm the kind of person who marks up her Bible. Are you too? Mine is highlighted and underlined. Dates and notes are in the margins. And I love running across scriptures I've circled, looking back at how God met me right where I was in that moment.

A few years ago my husband had my Bible rebound as a gift because it was literally falling apart. With all my notes in it, I couldn't bring myself to start fresh with a new one. I find endless encouragement as I flip through the story of my journey, marked up throughout that precious Book. And every time I open it, I'm reminded that God's words have the unique ability to show us our authentic selves.

Let's unpack a few characters from the Bible that were deeply affected by His words.

THE THIEF ON THE CROSS

As Jesus hung on the cross, He wasn't alone. A man hung on a cross on each side of Him. They were criminals facing consequences. As this scene in Luke 23 unfolded, the guards were drawing lots for Jesus' clothing. They were mocking Him, asking how He could save others when He couldn't save Himself.

But rather than lash out, defend His name, or step off that cross, Jesus uttered these famous words from verse 34: "Father, forgive them, for they don't know what they're doing" (VOICE). These ten words are laced with amazing grace and unconditional love.

Then one of the criminals spoke up. "You're supposed to be the Anointed One, right? Well—do it! Rescue Yourself and us" (v. 39 VOICE). But it was the criminal hanging on the other side of Jesus who defended Him. "We're getting what we deserve since we've committed crimes, but this man hasn't done anything wrong at all!" (v. 41 VOICE). He was beginning to see who he really was and what he really needed.

He then turned to Jesus and said, "When You come into Your kingdom, please remember me" (v. 42 VOICE). And in a sweet moment, Jesus promised him salvation that very day.

Chances are this thief had never heard the holy scrolls of God's Word read in the temple. But he did hear Jesus speak that day. He heard the words of God vocalized. And in those few hours of torment on the cross, being next to the

Word Himself, something shifted in his heart.

It changed his perspective.

It changed his understanding.

It changed his identity.

It changed his eternity.

Friend, that's what the Bible offers us even today.

DAVID

In 1 Samuel 30, David found himself in a hard place. He and his men had arrived back home at Ziklag, only to discover the Amalekites had attacked the city in their absence and taken their wives and children. Scripture says they wept until they were too exhausted to weep any longer. David's men directed their anger and grief toward him, and they even considered stoning him to satisfy their broken hearts.

In that moment, with his wives gone and his friends plotting his death, David was all alone. He had no one on his side. Verse 6 says, "But David felt strengthened and encouraged in the LORD his God" (AMP). This is a beautiful example of what God and His Word can do when we're weary. We don't need others to make us feel better; the Bible can do that for us.

You see, David didn't call a priest to speak life into his weary bones. He didn't try to phone a friend, looking for reassurance. He didn't turn to wine or food for inspiration or a mood boost. He reached out to God.

I'm sure he remembered God's faithfulness in his life. He probably thought about scripture read from the holy scrolls and remembered stories passed down that reiterated the Lord's trustworthiness. In that stressful moment, God's words gave him the grit and grace to find courage.

He knew who God made him to be, he knew who God called him to be, and David was unafraid to be his authentic self.

JOSHUA

After Moses died, God called Joshua to become the leader of the Israelites. He'd been Moses' number two, serving with him during their time in the wilderness. But now it was Joshua's turn to be number one. And as God passed the mantle to him, He urged Joshua to be authentic.

> *Always* be strong and courageous, *and always* live by all of the law *I gave to my servant Moses, never turning from it—even ever so slightly—so that you may succeed wherever you go. Let the words from the book of the law* be always on your lips. Meditate on them day and night *so that you may be careful to live by all that is written in it. If you do, as you make your way through this world, you will prosper and always find success.* (Joshua 1:7–8 VOICE, emphasis mine)

God's words were designed to change the way Joshua was thinking. They were giving him courage to rise and be who God made him to be. They were shifting his mind-set from second in command to the leader of God's children. The Lord was telling Joshua who he was and what he could do. God's words to him were laced with confidence-building tools, a challenge to live with authenticity, and they came with a built-in blessing for walking it out.

If you're struggling to know your authentic self, the Bible will reveal who you are. Everything you need to know about your identity—who God created you to be—can be found by camping in the Word of God. If you're afraid to be real in a world that glorifies the fake, scripture will help you find the grit and grace to unabashedly be yourself. If you need confidence to live honestly, verses in the Bible will strengthen your resolve.

I know the world's voice is loud. It's persuasive. It's telling us how we *should* look, how we *should* live, and who we *should* be. We're hearing about all the things we *should* be doing or what we *should* have. Friend, *should* is such a shaming word. And for many of us, it's overriding the words of God.

Let's take a quick time-out and review the last twenty-four hours. Think about all the *shoulds* that have come your way. Take an inventory of where you've felt like you haven't measured up or where you've failed to fit in. Perhaps society set a standard or the media created a yardstick or someone measured you against another, saying you *should*:

- ☐ Be better at something
- ☐ Volunteer more hours
- ☐ Have a better body
- ☐ Wear nicer clothes
- ☐ Earn more money
- ☐ Become a better cook
- ☐ Gain more followers on social media
- ☐ Get another degree
- ☐ Enhance your skills
- ☐ Turn into someone else
- ☐ _____ (fill in the blanks)
- ☐ _____
- ☐ _____

Sweet one, unless you and I spend time in the Word learning what God says is real and true and righteous, unless we know what God thinks of us right now, unless we see the truth of who we were created to be, unless we know what makes us shine, unless we see how the Word tells us to live and what qualities are important to God, unless we overcome our fear of the *shoulds*, we're going to live our lives covered in shame. And that will leave us discontent and discouraged.

That's not authentic living. Since God made you to shine, don't let anything or anyone make you afraid to be yourself. Do you know one surefire way to overcome the *shoulds*? Camp in the Word of God.

According to the latest State of the Bible survey by the American Bible Society,[16] as a nation we overwhelmingly consider the Bible to be a source of hope and a force for good. The report goes on to say that 81 percent of Americans think our moral fiber is fraying, saying the Bible is partly responsible for keeping positivity alive in our nation. But it gets even better.

When asked why they grabbed their Bibles, 68 percent of those interviewed said it was because it made them feel closer to God. And for the 39 percent who spent more time in the Word this past year, they admitted it was because of a difficult life experience. Even more, according to the *Guinness Book of World Records*, the Bible is still the highest-selling nonfiction book to date.[17] That must mean something, right? It's hard to deny that most of us consider camping in the Word a place of comfort, because it's where we find everything we need to live authentic in a world full of counterfeit everything.

Friend, the Bible is how we hear the heart of our heavenly Dad. It's the litmus test when we wonder if we're giving in to stinkin' thinkin'. It's the sword of the Spirit that helps us fight the Enemy's attacks against our self-worth. And it's our guide to live authentic lives pleasing to Him. Every day, we need God's Word to realign our hearts with His. In its pages we're supernaturally given life essentials. The Bible is our daily manna.

Matthew 6:11 says, "Give us *this day*, our daily bread" (AMP, emphasis mine). This is part of a prayer Jesus taught His followers to pray, and these seven words recognize our need for Him every day. If we ask, God will give us what we need—physically, emotionally, and spiritually. If we aren't camping in the Word every day, we are essentially starving ourselves.

God's Word is alive and active. Think about it. Have you ever read scripture so perfect for your situation that it jumped off the page and caught your attention? Or have you come across a familiar verse read in a different translation that brought it alive for you? Can you think of a time when a passage produced instant peace or comfort, or offered immediate resolve or strength to continue standing through the storm? These precious moments are conversations with your heavenly Father.

How can we live authentic lives if we don't connect regularly with the only One who knows us better than we know ourselves? How can we develop a solid self-worth when we're not sure who we are? How can we have confidence if we don't understand why we're valuable? How can we shine our genuine selves when we're unfamiliar with our light source? How can we find the courage not to give in to the world's counterfeit ways? How can we be effective when we don't recognize our purpose? *We can't.*

If you want to live an authentic life, the Bible is your solid foundation and detailed road map. It can help you be real in a world full of fake. It will never let you down. Its truth will never fall short. And the time you spend camping in the Word will never be wasted.

FINDING THE GRIT

What are your thoughts about the Bible?

We learn from 2 Timothy 3:16–17 that all scripture is God-breathed. Is this believable for you? Why or why not?

How have you seen God's Word encourage you or someone else?

What is your favorite translation or paraphrase of the Bible? Why?

What are some practical ways you can make camping in the Word more realistic with your busy schedule?

What Bible character's story spoke to you through this chapter?

What are your thoughts on our discussion of the *shoulds*?

How does camping in the Word of God help you live authentic?

FINDING THE GRACE

Father, thank You for inspiring others to write Your story. Thank You for creating a living, breathing document of Your faithfulness. I am choosing to believe that every word in Your book is true and useful for instruction. I know that it's foundational in my pursuit of authentic living, and I am asking You to help me create the habit of digging into its pages every day. I want to know You better, I want to know me better, and I know Your Word will help accomplish them both. Forgive me for not understanding the power of Your Holy Bible. Forgive me for shortchanging the truths inside. I want to be a woman who thrives from Your truths. Help me be a camper in Your Word. In Jesus' mighty name I pray, amen.

Live
Accept Your Awesomeness
Unearth the Untruths
Try Loving Everyone
Hold on to Hope
Embrace and Extend Forgiveness
Never Shrink Back
Trample the Negatives
Invest in Community
Camp in the Word of God

CHAPTER 13

Be Unafraid

It takes courage to grow up and become who you really are.
—E. E. Cummings[18]

$\mathcal{Y}$ou *are* brave.

Sometimes it might not feel that way. I get it. Trust me, I know it takes courage to be yourself. But His strength in you—through you—builds confidence to live authentic. And it's that confidence that concerns the Enemy.

You see, Satan authored fear. He owns it. It's one of his greatest and most powerful tools, and he uses it to keep you and me from being who God made us to be. The hope is that we'll partner with what we fear the most. We'll believe it. Then instead of living with self-confidence, rather than believing that who we are is good, we'll agree with the lies. And those lies will convince us to be anything but authentic. They'll influence us to be someone else. But, friend, fear is never from God.

Second Timothy 1:7 confirms it. "For God has not

given us a spirit of fear, but of power and of love and of a sound mind" (NKJV). This verse is from a letter Paul wrote to Timothy, and it was to be Paul's very last letter. Knowing all he knew based on his travels from sharing the Gospel, I love that Paul took this opportunity to remind his student to be unafraid. And while it was meant to encourage Timothy, it encourages me just as much. Maybe it will do the same for you.

As we venture to live authentic lives, let's unpack four powerful truths from this verse that will help keep fear at bay so we can be confident in who God made us to be.

1. God has not given us fear.

No fear we face is God-inspired. None of it. Not the fear of being exposed, nor the fear of not being enough, nor the fear of being unlovable, nor the fear of having our true selves rejected. Any fear we face is courtesy of the Enemy. Let's remember that.

2. God has given us power.

Praise the Lord, power isn't something we have to muster on our own. Any grit and grace we find to live authentic is only because of the power God has made available to us. We don't have to come up with it ourselves or handle our fears alone. You see, His power in us is readily available to us every time we need it.

3. God has given us His love.

And this love isn't based on our performance or being perfect. It has nothing to do with our past choices, our current season of sinning, or our future fears. God's love for us doesn't waver if we hate ourselves or are covered in shame. He can't love us any more or any less than He does right now. God's love is unchangeable and complete.

Even more, his perfect love casts out fear according to 1 John 4:18. We don't have to be afraid to be ourselves, even when it feels risky to do so.

4. God has given us sound minds.

Every day we process a billion different thoughts. Some of these thoughts build confidence, but so often we're bombarded with ones that strip it right from us. It's no surprise that our minds can be a breeding ground for fearful thoughts that create self-doubt. The Enemy loves to whisper lies that fester in our minds, keeping us from authentic living. But Paul tells us it doesn't have to be this way.

We have direct access to God's strength of mind. In those moments when we need God to bring our thoughts into alignment with His, we can go to Him. This constant renewal is available to us anytime we need it. All we have to do is ask God to remind us of who we are and whose we are.

Paul shared this powerful reminder to be unafraid because he was fully aware of the Enemy's plans. He knew Satan wants to scare us into counterfeit living, paralyzed from being the women God made us to be. Why is he so bent on this torment? Well, it's because he hates you and the call your heavenly Father has placed on your life.

In 1 Peter 5:8, we get a clearer understanding of who we're dealing with and what he wants to do. It reads, "Be well balanced (temperate, sober of mind), be vigilant and cautious at all times; for that enemy of yours, the devil, roams around like a lion roaring [in fierce hunger], seeking someone to seize upon and devour" (AMPC). And while that sounds utterly frightening, knowing that he is out for our blood, it makes sense.

I'd like to suggest that his greatest fear is that you and I will fully embrace our identities as children of God. The Enemy is on a rampage to create self-doubt because he understands that if we step into the truth of who we are, we'll be a force to be reckoned with. Satan is scared to death of who we may become in the future. And that is why every attack we face is designed to shut us up and shut us down.

When I was sexually abused by a stranger at the age of four, I didn't tell a soul for eight years. In that time, the Enemy's lies knotted my self-worth into a million tangles of insecurity. It left me doubting my value. And I limped into adulthood, afraid I had nothing to offer. I was scared I'd never be fully loved. I was fearful, unable to trust the kindness of others. That abuse left me hypervigilant, constantly anxious that someone else was going to hurt me. And rather than find the grit and grace to be who God made me to be, I cowered. For most of my life, I was anything but authentic.

It may have looked like I was open and honest, but every bit of information I divulged was calculated. I shared only what felt safe, what I deemed appropriate or acceptable. Fear ruled me to my core, making me believe I was worthless and unlovable. And any hint of confidence was a façade. My I'm-not-good-enough fears convinced me to hide my true self from everyone. And the Enemy patted himself on the back.

Maybe you've done that too. Chances are life has beaten the self-assurance right out of you. And like me, you've allowed lie-based fears to keep your authentic self tucked away. But that's not the way God wants us to live.

When God thought you up, it delighted Him. He wasn't in a bad mood when He made you. God didn't form you because He needed to fill space on the earth. Friend, you're an intentional creation, and He put time and effort into your design. You really are fearfully and wonderfully made, just like we're told in Psalm 139:14.

In the original Hebrew, the word *fearfully* means (1) with great reverence, (2) with a heartfelt interest, and (3) with respect. And the word *wonderfully* means (1) unique, (2) set-apart, and (3) marvelous.[19] These words describe how you were created and who you are to God. This is your authentic self. Even if the world tells you otherwise, this is the *real* you.

Through all the battles I've faced in my life, I've learned that when fear is connected to something, it's often because the Enemy wants to keep you from it. Chances are something beautiful and amazing is on the other side that he doesn't want you to possess. And if the Enemy can keep you trapped in counterfeit living—too afraid to be yourself—you're divinely designed future will never come to be. He will have effectively neutralized you.

But, friend, your calling is on the other side of all your fears. Stepping into your calling with the power and authority available to you requires your authenticity. You must be willing to embrace who God created you to be. It's not a call to be perfect, but purposeful. And when you let Him fill you with courage, untangle knots of insecurity, and cancel lies telling you to hide your true self from the world, God will bring you into a new space.

This new space is full of confidence to be yourself no matter what anyone else thinks. It gives you the boldness to live unafraid, even when criticism and judgment come your way. And while you'll most certainly be afraid to live authentic from time to time, this new space helps you muster the grit and grace to war against that fear rather than give in to it.

Sweet one, God made you to be real with Him, yourself, and others. Something inside of you is meant to be shared with the world—and it takes confidence to release it. God has baked something into you meant to introduce the saving power of Jesus to those around you. And it's all on the other side of fear.

It's normal to feel afraid, but we can't live afraid. It's not who God made you to be or how He wants you to live.

The One who made you on purpose—your heavenly Father who fully loves you, the Divine Designer who delights in His beautiful creation—wants you to

Be you.

Be authentic.

And find the grit and grace to shine.

Notes

1. "Quotes about Fake," goodreads.com, accessed October 22, 2017, https://www.goodreads.com/quotes/tag/fake.

2. Merriam-Webster, s.v. "condemn," accessed October 22, 2017, https://www.merriam-webster.com/dictionary/condemn.

3. "Quotes about Authenticity," goodreads.com, accessed October 22, 2017, https://www.goodreads.com/quotes/tag/authenticity.

4. "Authentic," dictionary.com, accessed December 14, 2017, http://www.dictionary.com/browse/authentic.

5. "Sunday Adelaja," goodreads.com, accessed December 14, 2017, https://www.goodreads.com/quotes/search?utf8=%E2%9C%93&q=you+will+not+be+capable+of+living+your+own+life.+++%E2%80%95Sunday+Adelaja&commit=Search.

6. "Quotes about Self-Acceptance," goodreads.com, accessed May 15, 2017, http://www.goodreads.com/quotes/tag/self-acceptance.

7. "Brené Brown," goodreads.com, accessed July 23, 2017, https://www.goodreads.com/quotes/631488-because-true-belonging-only-happens-when-we-present-our-authentic.

8. "Quotes about Lies," goodreads.com, accessed July 23, 2017, http://www.goodreads.com/quotes/tag/lies.

9. "Strongs Greek.5544.Chréstotés," Biblehub.com, accessed December 14, 2017, http://biblehub.com/greek/5544.htm.

10. "Ziad K. Abdelnour," goodreads.com, accessed Februay 26, 2018, https//www.goodreads.com/quotes/971721-forget-all-the-reasons-why-it-won-t-work-and-believe.

11. "Martin Luther King Jr," goodreads.com, accessed October 31, 2017, https://www.goodreads.com/quotes/57037-forgiveness-is-not-an-occasional-act-it-is-a-constant.

12. "Thomas Edison," brainyquote.com, accessed October 31, 2017, https://www.brainyquote.com/quotes/thomas_a_edison_149049.

13. "Ralph Marston," AZ Quotes, accessed February 26, 2018, www.azquotes.com/quote/849734.

14. "Helen Keller," goodreads.com, accessed November 9, 2017, https://www.goodreads.com/quotes/9411-alone-we-can-do-so-little-together-we-can-do.

15. "Charles Haddon Spurgeon," goodreads.com, accessed January 20, 2017, https://www.goodreads.com/quotes/397346-a-bible-that-s-falling-apart-usually-belongs-to-someone-who.

16. American Bible Society, "Americans Say Nation's Morals are Declining but Believe Bible Is Foundation of Hope," American Bible Society News, April4, 2017, http://news.americanbible.org/blog/entry/corporate-blog/americans-say-nations-morals-are-declining-but-believe-bible-is-foundation.

17. "Bestselling Book of Non-fiction," Guinnessworldrecords.com, accessed October 12, 2017, http://www.guinness-worldrecords.com/world-records/best-selling-book-of-non-fiction.

18. "e. e. Cummings quotes," brainyquote.com, accessed November 9, 2017, https://www.brainyquote.com/quotes/e_e_cummings_161593.

19. Dan Downey, "Fearfully and Wonderfully Made," savedhealed.com, accessed December 14, 2017, http://www.savedhealed.com/fearfully.htm.